Tiny Space Gardening

Tiny Space Gardening

Growing Vegetables, Fruits, and Herbs in Small Outdoor Spaces (with Recipes)

Amy Pennington

SASQUATCH BOOKS
SEATTLE

Contents

Introduction

I am an urban gardener. Some may think of me as an urban farmer, depending on how you differentiate between a farm and a garden. I grow food for people in their city backyards, front yards, side yards, you name it: any patch of land in which I can persuade food to grow. And by food, I mean greens, roots, fruits, herbs, flowers, and more. My hope is to inspire people to eat a broader range of food and flavors than they are used to. I also want to evoke a sort of small-scale self-sufficiency in the daily lives of urbanites. I like food and living green, so I want to have a steady supply of fresh, delicious produce as often as possible. I am motivated by my hunger, and so I grow food.

The ironic thing about my story is that, at present, I do not actually have a garden of my own. I live in a small apartment in Seattle with no access to a backyard, a lawn, or even green space. And though I often dream of tearing up my assigned parking spot and building a raised vegetable bed in its place, I don't think my landlord would appreciate the effort. So like most city people in search of greener pastures, I make do with what I have: in my case, an east-facing deck that gets the first rays of morning sun. Over time, I have overcrowded this tiny 75-square-foot space with pots, containers, hanging baskets, window boxes, and more. (I also use my dining room table as a greenhouse in the winter, which means inviting plants to further encroach on what little personal space I have.) I originally started with flowers and killed a good number of them. I now know that I wasn't watering efficiently, or the pots were too small, but at the time I just chalked it up to a big experiment.

My relationship with plants changed when I was asked to build and plant an organic vegetable garden for a food-loving Seattle couple. They hoped to grow the same tomatoes their nonna had grown in Italy. While I had little firsthand knowledge on how best to do this, I thought it sounded like an awesome challenge, so I dug in. Putting my hands in the dirt for the first time and sowing seeds was immediately very natural for me. I remember looking up at my friend Marcus (who worked with me that first year) and saying, "Marcus, this is the most instinctual thing I've ever done." I didn't have to think about it. I just planted. And like most new gardeners, I was shocked and amazed when those little green seedlings started pushing out of the soil. Nearly everything came up that year, and the garden was a huge success.

From then on, I was officially a grow-your-own convert, and I started experimenting with all sorts of plants. I grew spices, ate flowers, sowed Asian greens (some names of which I still can't pronounce), tried ten varieties of paste tomatoes, and more. The more time I spent in the garden, the more obvious the life cycle of plants became. I learned what it meant to overwater or underwater. I did plant trials in each of the raised beds to see how sun patterns would affect growth. All in all, I became really good at growing food efficiently and maximizing space. It was like a little game I played with myself—*how much food can I grow in this small space in the shortest amount of time?*

After that first year (and after getting used to bringing home some of that garden's bounty), I quickly tired of running across town to clip a handful of thyme for dinner. I refused to buy herbs at the grocery when I had fresh herbs to pick, but the back-and-forth car trips demanded too much energy. I disliked having to plan meals too far ahead, and being environmentally minded, I felt guilty for burning the fuel. In the course of a summer, I slowly transitioned all of the flower pots at my apartment into containers of edible plants. Today, my deck overflows with pots, soil, and plants. I still have a thyme plant from that first garden thriving in a big pot on my balcony. I didn't really think about the transition happening just outside my door—it just happened organically.

In truth, I have grown food and plants far longer than my short adult history would suggest. I grew up in the wilds of Long Island in New York. My parents had defected from Brooklyn and Queens to live a simple life out in the "country." And although my childhood home sat within spitting distance of the Long Island Expressway, it really did feel like country. Our house was tucked in at the edge of a dead-end street. The yard was backed by a few acres of wooded land with meandering trails. The front yard started off like any old front yard, full of willow trees and a green lawn to run and do somersaults across, but over time my dad transitioned it to a working homestead. He built a gated pen for milk goats and another one for our pig, Maggie. We had rabbits for meat up in hutches, and one year we raised commercial turkeys for Thanksgiving, selling them to all his city friends. Muscovy ducks just sort of wandered around the yard, laying eggs where they saw fit. We would clip their wings every couple of months because if we didn't, they had a tendency to fly up and perch on the neighbor's roof. There was a large coop for the chickens, though they had free rein and could easily be corralled back to the coop at night.

In the backyard sat my parents' pride and joy: a huge vegetable garden. I remember my father renting a rototiller and turning over the turf one summer. As kids, we were utterly uninterested, but looking back now, I think my parents were superheroes. They tilled up the grass and hoed in rows like real farmers. No raised beds, no fancy "garden," just row after row of vegetables. I have pictures of them hunched over rows of beans, while we kids are sitting in the shade in bathing suits doing nothing. Looking back now, I see that it was also one big adventurous experiment for my parents. Like most new gardeners, we had far too many zucchini. My dad would send us round the neighborhood to pawn them off on other families. I was so embarrassed once when I was refused. Tomatoes came in excess, sunflowers got eaten by birds (and their seeds did *not* taste like sunflower seeds from the store, so we snubbed them), and snap peas were my favorite.

My brother, sister, and I had weekly chores that, like most children, we dreaded. Unlike most of our friends with standard-issue duties, our burgeoning homestead kept us busy collecting eggs, milking the goats, tending to the other animals, and working in the vegetable garden out back. You can imagine the chore list, come weekends. Someone had to clean out the goat shed, someone had to turn the compost pile we kept in the chicken coop, and someone had to weed. I remember sitting on a small bench in the garden and ripping out weeds, leaving some roots behind, and feeling both guilty and utterly empowered. I smugly left small pieces of dandelion root, knowing they would come back again to taunt us. (Sorry, Dad!) Above all other chores, I hated working in the garden.

While I hated garden work as a kid, I clearly found my calling as an adult. These days, I can be found in a garden any given day of the week, and I am continually drawing on my youth as a reference point. I wouldn't trade the way my parents raised me for the world.

I've been growing food in containers off my balcony for over ten years since the first edition of this book was published, and I've adjusted what I spend my time and effort cultivating. Today, I grow a collection of herbs—these are usually perennial plants that flower in midsummer, so they're both beautiful and delicious. While I used to steer clear of tomatoes (too much work!), I can appreciate the appeal of having a handful of those sweet red fruits to eat each summer, and this new version of the book has loads of information on how to grow healthy tomato plants.

Along with tomatoes, I've expanded my list of things to grow in containers and included some crowd favorites like basil, potatoes, and berries of all kinds. You'll also find more recipes to enjoy your harvest, as well as some easy windowsill and countertop projects. I absolutely adore sprouting seeds and think it's such an easy way to grow food at home even if you don't have access to outdoor space. I'll be making loads of sprouts this year. That said, I do have a shared rooftop garden with tall container beds that receive full sun all year long. I'm looking forward to discovering what I'll cook up next.

Before You Begin:
The Basics

Over the years, I have experimented with growing food in pots and containers. Living in a small apartment with limited space has forced me to get creative. You know that expression, "Necessity is the mother of invention"? Well, my friend Jason Werle says, "Frustration is the mother of invention," and I couldn't agree more! I'll be the first to admit, pots are not my favorite way to grow food. But they work well enough, and I certainly can't complain about fresh salad greens just outside my door.

Contrary to recent popular belief, though, not all vegetables grow well in containers. Most plants can be grown in a pot; however, not all plants will come to full maturity and produce food when grown in a pot. By planting in a pot you are inhibiting the plant's growth to some extent. Plants can send out roots and root hairs only as far as the walls of the pot allow. This presents the biggest challenge of growing food in small spaces. Growing food in pots and containers calls for a different mind-set than you need for growing food in the ground. However, armed with a little bit of information you can make educated decisions and increase your chances of success.

We tend to think about the dirt under our feet as just that—dirt. But soil is another matter. Without healthy soil, we would not be able to grow food. Natural soil is a living thing, with inherent qualities that are not readily available in a bag of potting soil. Potassium, nitrogen, microbial matter, phosphates, calcium, and other nutrients are present in natural soil in varying degrees. Soil breathes, grows, lives—and can die. Hundreds of articles have been written about the importance of healthy soil on a global level, and you should read them. Soil is crucial to our livelihood.

When you're growing food (or any plant) in a container, however, you don't use soil. Instead, you use a potting mix—also called a soil *medium*. The density of this mix is lighter than garden soil and conditioned for containers. Therefore, container gardens run the risk of lacking all of those healthy minerals and living organisms that naturally occur in soil. To be a successful container gardener, you have to really think like a plant.

For a new gardener, it is helpful to recognize that information often varies from source to source. Also, it's good to note that gardening "experts" often use a combination of education and experience to offer advice and instruction on how to grow a bountiful garden. That doesn't necessarily mean it will all work for you. I have opinions about what works and what doesn't, but there are many options for home gardeners. Gardening means working with nature, and this is not an exact science. There are far too many variables to be able to definitively state what will grow best where. Sun exposure, latitude, time of year, watering schedule—all of these things and more will affect the success of any planting you do. It depends on what you have to work with and your own preferences. For instance, I didn't grow tomato plants in my previous apartment garden. Tomatoes need big pots, and my deck was already too small. Also, tomatoes are sun lovers, and I don't get enough sun. Even in the *best* conditions I would harvest only a few pints of cherry tomatoes from one plant. With all the nurturing and time that tomatoes need, it's just not worth it to me to bother. Especially when farmers' markets abound and I can pick up locally grown tomatoes each summer. So although certain factual information about nutrient requirements won't change among the many books you can read, strategies will. It's up to you to decide what works best for you and your garden—and like me, you will learn your best lessons from experiments and experience.

Here I have distilled my cumulative experience in a variety of conditions over time in the hopes that this information will help you make good choices. You should read up on all the science-y stuff too. This books offers a basic overview of the important elements to gardening. To problem solve, you need to understand a plant's needs and why it behaves in certain ways. Although plants do a really good job of keeping themselves alive, it's smart to understand what is happening and how you can help them along. This foundation of basic knowledge is a great place to start.

In general, I take a fairly lazy approach to any apartment garden. The ultimate goal is for the garden to be productive. I want a constant supply of the ingredients I use often, and I want to nurture plants that can be continually harvested from. I want both plants that will run through their life cycle in one season as well as plants that are perennials and will continue to come back year after year. I try to mix reseeding plants and perennials with those annuals that must be planted anew each year, so I'm not starting completely from scratch every spring. It's a satisfying experience to see your garden getting started before you've even had time to think about planting and planning. *That* is the best kind of apartment garden: one that isn't too high-maintenance and can fend for itself when need be, all the while offering up fresh ingredients for your kitchen. Brilliant.

A successful apartment garden requires some thought and strategy. I often say choosing what to grow on my deck is like the *Sophie's Choice* of gardening—an impossible decision that must be made. I suggest growing plants that will be used frequently, but in small amounts. This gives plants time to regrow between cuttings. No sense in planting a crop that you'll wipe out in one go. I figure it's better to have something available over a long course of time. To that end, I rely heavily on herbs for the apartment garden.

Herbs will single-handedly change the flavor of most recipes. Eaten fresh, or cooked over time, they impart a flavor that few other foods can. They are the quintessential kitchen ingredients, and the choices extend far beyond the commonly used thyme, rosemary, and sage.

I also grow plants that produce abundant quantities of ingredients that I know I'll use often. Lettuces, for example: these are wonderful to grow at home. They take up little space, produce (and reproduce!) quickly, and offer fresh greens for salads or a nice leafy garnish. I use lettuce in large amounts, and their leaves grow back quickly, making them highly productive, economical, and worthwhile. There are few other vegetable plants that work especially well in containers, but there are a handful that are ideal for the small working space of apartment gardens.

Make the most of what you grow by considering its uses beyond the kitchen. Scented geranium leaves can be chopped and used with sweet recipes, and they can also be infused into a tea. Some plants are grown for leaves, some for seeds, and some for fruits. I try to round out my garden plan so there is always something to harvest from. Today, as I write this, I have lovage seeds, anise hyssop, nigella (love-in-a-mist), and scented geraniums. In three weeks the nigella will be gone, the lovage will be cut back, and I'll be harvesting a second crop of lettuce. A container garden should ebb and flow, just as a large garden would.

Having an apartment garden likely means your space is small. Outside of begging your neighbors for some prime deck real estate, take advantage of the wider urban garden available to you every day. Outside the confines of your compact garden lies a city full of wild edibles that often go neglected and undiscovered. When strolling about your city, keep your eyes peeled. You likely won't have to travel far to find something edible growing close by.

Look on the ground: windfalls from abandoned fruit and nut trees and wild greens are ready and accessible nearly all year long. Although foraging is a craft honed over time, anyone can spot and pick out a dandelion from a grassy field. Start your foraging adventures small. Pick what you know with 100 percent certainty. Pretty soon, you'll be doing homework and gathering more plants to eat. Knowledge is an evolution, and nature provides the perfect seasonal time line to learn from.

And really, that is what it's all about. Learning while you go. And grow! This book is meant as a beginner's guide, with everything you need to get started. All the plants you'll learn about here are easy, low bars for entry to gardening; some projects don't even require potting soil—and will have you eating in days. They may not be the most often-suggested edible plants, but they're all tasty and beautiful and seasonal and charming. I hope you'll dig in to one of these small projects now, and next year or next season you'll dig a little deeper. Trial and error are your best guides, particularly as no two gardens are created equal. Make the most of your space and see what happens.

And, most importantly, don't fret. Plants *want* to survive and live. They will go to great lengths to make sure their genetic strain lives on. They are genetically predisposed to grow big and strong so they can set seed and make more plants. They don't need constant monitoring—they just need a helper.

Have fun, do your best, and I bet you'll come out smelling like roses. And you know what? If you're just dying to grow a tomato on your patio, you should definitely go for it.

Garden Glossary 101

Here are some gardening terms to familiarize yourself with, as well as some professional vocabulary that you should know before you get started.

AMENDMENT: A beneficial ingredient added to the soil: fertilizer, compost, sand, and so on.

ANNUAL: A plant that completes its life cycle in one season or year. Annuals must be reseeded (naturally or intentionally) in order to grow in subsequent years.

CLOCHE: A protective covering made of material, glass, or plastic meant to promote and foster healthy plant growth.

COTYLEDON: The first tiny leaves that develop on a seedling after germination.

DEADHEADING: To remove dead flower heads from a plant

HARDENING OFF: Slowly acclimating new plants to outdoor weather conditions by putting them outside for increasing lengths of time.

OVERWINTER: The duration of time from fall to spring for plants that can survive outside unprotected. Overwintering also refers to the process of putting plants under protective cover so they may survive the winter.

PERENNIAL: A plant that lives longer than one growing season, typically for more than two years.

PHOTOTROPISM: When a plant bends toward a light source.

RESEEDING ANNUAL: An annual plant that drops seed on its own, thereby self-sowing for the following year.

ROGUE GARDENING: The act of dropping seed bombs or tossing seeds into open places, hoping they will germinate and grow on their own.

ROOT-BOUND: Condition of a plant that has outgrown its pot, so its roots press against the container walls and twist around each other.

RUNNER: A plant that will send out roots from its stem to produce another plant that can be severed from the parent plant. Strawberries spread by runners.

TOP-DRESS: To dress the top layer of soil, surrounding a plant with fertilizer, mulch, or compost.

Getting Grounded:
Pots, Containers, Soil, and Supplies

For beginning gardeners, or even those with a year or two under their belt, the world of garden tools, materials, and supplies can be overwhelming. I have stood in the garden aisles of home stores and nurseries, utterly baffled by the multitude of products available. I cannot imagine what it must feel like to try to sort through all that information and decide what essentials you need to get started and get growing.

The good news is you really don't need much, particularly for a smaller container garden. Before you invest too much in supplies, determine whether your deck gets at least a few hours of sun. Ambient light may be OK to grow some herbs and potentially a lettuce or two, but you can kiss any thoughts of cucumbers and tomatoes goodbye. Sorry! And if you really don't get a lick of sun, check out your community gardening programs. Most cities offer up plots in community gardens, and often a neighbor is more than happy to share part of a yard. If, however, you have a minimum of six hours of sunlight, the world of edibles opens up to you. Tomatoes would still be a challenge, but herbs, leafy greens, and some fruiting plants like snap peas will grow.

To start a garden in containers, at a bare minimum you'll need pots, soil, and fertilizer. A bag of compost is a great addition, so you should purchase one of those when you're gathering supplies. (And see the Feeding and Watering Plants chapter, page 91.) Access to water is also an important consideration. In my own garden, I fill old water bottles and carry them back and forth from my kitchen sink. In an apartment, it's usually not too far of a carry! Just make sure you have some way to water your plants, as containers require a diligent watering schedule. Small container gardens benefit from a few other supplies as well. These extras support your plants, help to prolong the growing season, and generally make your life a little easier.

You might think choosing pots would be the easiest part of an apartment garden, but interestingly, it is not. Containers and pots come in many sizes and shapes and seemingly just as many materials. You can look at your planting vessel in one of two ways—you can choose the pot first and then pick the best-suited plant, or buy the plant and then choose the best-suited pot. I find myself consistently drawn to cute little pots with bright colors, but they end up being fairly useless for growing food. Most plants need legroom to stretch their roots. Try to plant in a pot that's a bit bigger than the plant will actually need. It is better to leave a little wiggle room than to have plant roots mashing up against the container walls. I always go big—if you allow for some growth, you increase the odds of your plant growing to full maturity. The goal is for the plant to produce as much as possible. In What to Grow for a Plentiful Harvest (page 33), there are notes under each plant suggesting the most ideal container. Decide for yourself and know that everything is an experiment. You can always adjust next year, or transplant later in the season if you've underestimated.

If you have the energy and creativity to make your own containers, go for it. Building a custom-made container gives you much more flexibility, as you ultimately control the width and depth. I prefer angular containers like squares and rectangles. Their linear shape allows for row planting, even if on a small scale. This chapter has some basic instructions for a simple planter box. Traditional round pots tend to taper at the bottom, which helps with drainage but also crams the roots together. All in all, shoot for an equal mix of both container shapes.

Container material is an area where you need to make some personal choices. I love the look and feel of terra-cotta clay pots. They are uniform and shapely. They also come in a multitude of different sizes, so you can overcrowd small spaces with a variety of plants in a way that's pleasing to the eye. The consistency and repetition of the same pot ties the varied collection together and gives a tidy appearance. Ceramic pots are a great option as well. They are typically glazed and add a bit of color to the garden. The downside of ceramic pots is that they can cost twice as much as their terra-cotta counterparts. But when you are working in a small garden, aesthetics are important, so go ahead and add a touch of vibrancy here and there—just don't spend your entire budget on pots alone. One important note about ceramic pots: if you buy one without a drainage hole, have the nursery drill several, or make your own using an electric drill (see Hand-Drilled Drainage, page 12). Plants generally need good drainage to grow well; without it, a pot can easily get waterlogged, air doesn't circulate as readily, and it's hard to tell when the plant needs more water.

Hand-Drilled Drainage

If you start looking around town for various containers you can use on your patio for planters, you will likely find some pretty cool things. Among the jackpot items are ceramic pots. Glazed ceramic pots are more expensive then terra-cotta, so I rarely spend the money on them, but they add a splash of color and are so pretty they're hard to resist. But from time to time people do give these away. Just keep your eyes peeled. In the event that there are no drainage holes in these pots (which is often the case), you can actually drill your own. You need an electric drill and a special bit, but if you don't have your own set of electric tools, borrow them from someone and you're golden. The bigger the pot, the more holes you should have. Three to five per each pot is usually fine.

Here's how to drill drainage holes. Flip the pot over onto a lawn or a few layers of newspaper. (You want a soft surface to cushion the pot so you don't chip the edges.) Cover the area where you will drill the holes with a crisscross of masking tape. This helps to prevent splinters from flying up. Mark the holes on the tape. Using a drill fitted with either a ceramic or masonry bit, drill your hole. Try to drill straight down in one swift motion to minimize the chance of cracking the ceramic.

POTS AND CONTAINERS

Sizes

Staring up at the walls of pots available for gardening can be a bit daunting. Don't freak out! Any old pot is better than no pot, though it is helpful to make a plan before you go shopping. Pots come in a variety of shapes and sizes and can be grouped simply into large, medium, and small. Keep those general terms in mind and make sure to pick up a variety of pots. Purchase one or two pots at a time to add to your garden. This gives you time to adjust to general garden care without being overwhelmed and spaces out your budget over several seasons.

LARGE POTS

I categorize large pots as those deeper than 16 inches. Typically, both round pots and square containers come in widths proportionate to their depths. Larger pots will expand your gardening possibilities, as they offer enough space for larger plants to grow in—so I say go big and try something a bit larger than what you had in mind. When purchasing large pots, opt for the largest one they have. For a visual cue, make a circle in front of your body with your arms, fingertips touching. This width is about the diameter of a large pot. If you ever come across a large pot that someone is giving away, nab it! If you purchase a *really* large container, as you would do for an apple tree, consider also purchasing a plant trolley—a small platform on wheels—so you're able to move the pot with ease, if necessary.

MEDIUM POTS

Medium-sized pots run between 8 and 16 inches deep. Long, shallow pots are also considered medium-sized due to the reasonable amount of space they allow for growing. Most people choose medium pots, but this size should really be used only for smaller plants such as lettuce or mâche, or creeping herbs like thyme.

SMALL POTS

These little one-plant pots are less than 8 inches deep. I fill small, dainty pots with hardy herbs or single lettuce plants, accepting that they won't fully mature. Small pots are great for adding color and dimension to the garden and can be used to grow microgreens. In my experience, it's easy to be tempted into buying more small pots than you really need; remember, you can always go back for more.

Materials

PLASTIC

Plastic pots are the least expensive container option, so they're great for anyone on a budget. It's true that they are usually the least attractive option, and they do not weather in that lovely rustic way that ceramic pots do. On the plus side, however, plastic pots will hold their moisture longer than clay or ceramic pots. And plastic planters are lighter and easier to move around. I grow my lettuces in a long, narrow, shallow plastic pot that I gussy up with a coat of bright spray paint.

CLAY

Clay pots are porous, so air moves easily through their walls. This is helpful in that it allows roots to breathe and keeps them out of direct water, but it's not helpful in that the soil tends to dry out quickly. In hot weather you'll need to closely monitor the moisture in your clay pots. These pots are a fairly inexpensive option for the home gardener, after plastic ones, and they come in myriad shapes and sizes. If you choose clay pots, be sure to purchase a saucer or plate to set under the pot. This works in two ways—to keep moisture off the surface of your deck or patio and to hold a bit of moisture for the plant.

Small Plants for Small Pots

I'd like to reiterate that the size of the container will eventually affect the size a plant will grow. I'm not a huge fan of small pots for growing anything edible. The plants may not die, but certainly many will not come to full maturity if you inhibit their space in this way. Small pots will also dry out very quickly. In my own garden, the smallest pot I have used was about four inches deep and about that wide—I treated it as an experiment. Nothing really grew well in such a small space, and what little of the plant was alive was horribly root-bound, poor thing. Even lettuces, which are pretty tolerant, suffered in such tight confines. Their leaves never got bigger than baby lettuce size, and I wound up scrapping the whole project.

Very few plants grow well in these conditions, but there are a few you can get away with. The smallest pot I would recommend would be 6 inches deep and about the same width. This size pot can accommodate one small plant. Just one! I can't tell you how many plants I've seen crammed into these tiny pots, and I

WOOD

Wooden boxes, whether purchased or built, are nice additions to the patio garden. They are perfectly angular and therefore easy to grow in and fit neatly into corners. They come in large sizes that give plants plenty of space. Wood withstands weathering over time, and even if the edges become slightly warped or dull, the plants in them will grow. I have had the same wooden boxes for well over seven years now, and they're still in decent shape. As with clay, the growing medium in wooden boxes will dry out a bit faster than in plastic, but the wood, being porous, does tend to hold moisture a smidge longer.

promise you—they will not grow. (Unless you plan on going the microgreen route [see page 173], in which you harvest plant starts when they are only 1 to 2 inches tall. In that case, you can fill the pot with seeds and generally harvest within two weeks.)

In small pots, shallow-rooted plants work best. Small pots can also accommodate plants that you do not need to harvest from often. Lemon balm, for instance, is quite hardy and will survive the tight conditions, though its leaves will be much smaller than those of a plant given room to reach its full potential. This doesn't matter so much for lemon balm, as it is a strong herb that you're not likely to use frequently. Keep in mind, also, that small pots need lots of watering on hot days—likely at least twice a day.

The following is a list of some good plant options for smaller pots—as they are either shallow-rooted or a kind of plant you will not use in large quantities and can harvest in smaller batches.

- Lemon balm
- Microgreens: arugula, radish
- Scented mints: chocolate, pineapple, apple
- Strawberry

Build a Planter Box

This simple design is based on one large sheet of plywood, enough to make two smaller boxes. Plywood is not the strongest or best wood you can use for planter box materials, but it's cheap and functional. These boxes are built with the notion that you'll use them for only a couple of years before moving on to greener pastures, literally. I have designed these planter boxes to sit up on casters (wheels that attach to the underside) so you can roll them around as needed, and the space beneath the box allows for good drainage.

This is an easy afternoon project, but listen up: when you go to cut your lumber, you must cut it in a specific sequence, because something kooky will happen as you cut the wood. When you cut lumber, you'll need to keep in mind something called a *kerf*. The kerf refers to the narrow proportion of wood you lose from the original piece from the width of the saw blade. In this instance the blade being used is generally ⅛-inch thick. To compensate for this loss, I have laid out a sequence of cuts to follow that take the kerf into account. In doing so, you will end up with a few small pieces of scrap lumber. Use them for signs or some other creative project.

The easiest way to get this job done and done right is to have your lumberyard cut the sections for you. Plywood is big and heavy and will need clamping and blocking in order to cut it properly. In short, it's a real hassle.. Choose a lumberyard over a home improvement store. Most lumberyard staff have long experience in adeptly cutting their products to order.

You have options for the type of plywood you choose. The lumberyard staff should be able to walk you through your choices.

Be sure to purchase plywood that is ¾-inch thick. Aside from that, the exterior grade I recommend is very rough and made to withstand the elements, but the surface will not be smooth. If you want a nice smooth finish because you intend to paint the exterior, choose a sanded plywood, which is slightly more expensive.

MATERIALS

- One sheet plywood—48 by 96 inches, ¾-inch thick, exterior grade

  Cut into:
  - Four pieces of 35 by 15 inches
  - Four pieces of 12 by 15 inches
  - Two pieces of 36.5 by 12 inches

- Thirty-two screws, ¾-inch-long (be sure to match the size of the screw to the hole in the caster so it holds the caster in place properly)
- Eighty-four 1¾-inch-long coarse thread, exterior-grade decking screws
- Eight heavy-duty casters, each with 100 pounds capacity
- Danish or orange oil

DIRECTIONS

1 Separate your materials into two equal sets so that you have the same materials for each of your beds.

2 Enlist a friend to help you balance all of these pieces. On a flat and level work surface, stand a 35-by-15-inch piece of plywood on one long side. Stand up a 12-by-15-inch piece of plywood against the **outside edge** of the longer piece, matching up the 15-inch sides. Have your friend hold the two pieces snugly and squarely together. Next, drill 4 evenly spaced pilot holes to accommodate the screws. (A pilot hole is an initial smaller hole made in wood using a smaller drill bit, thereby preventing splitting when you →

drill in the screws.) Using a ³⁄₃₂-inch drill bit, drill through the 12-by-15-inch piece into the larger piece. Try to drill as straight as possible, centering in the ¾-inch thickness, so you don't poke out of the side. After you've piloted the holes, screw the 2 pieces together using the 1¾-inch coarse thread decking screws. You now have the front and one side of the box attached.

3 Stand the other piece of 12-by-15-inch plywood against the opposite end of the longer piece, on its **outside edge**. Drill four pilot holes and screw together as on the other end. Fit the other 35-by-15-inch piece of plywood between the two side pieces and pilot and screw together in the same manner. Be sure to complete one side before moving to the last side. You now should have a bottomless wooden box frame.

4 Next, decide which side will be the top and which the bottom. You want the bottom to be the side where all the corners best match up and lie nice and flat. Once you've chosen, flip the box upside down, so the bottom is facing up. Place a 36½-by-12-inch piece over the box to form the bottom. Evenly space 9 screws along each long edge and 4 along each short edge. Working your way around the edge, pilot and then screw the bottom on.

5 Next, drill drainage holes into the bottom of the box using a ³⁄₈-inch drill bit. You will make two rows of holes every 4 inches across the bottom. There should be nine holes in each row. Space the rows 4 inches from the sides of the box. This should be adequate drainage.

6   Before you complete the box, add the casters to the corners of the bottom. Place each caster so its edge lines up with the edge of the box, make a smaller pilot hole, and screw in place with the shorter ¾-inch screws.

7   Your boxes will last longer if you apply a thin coat of oil before planting. Oil helps give the wood a tough and slightly waterproof finish. Apply two coats, letting each dry overnight, before filling with soil and planting.

8   To build the second box, repeat these steps!

SALVAGED MATERIALS

Every year, I email a local restaurant and ask them to set aside some asparagus crates for me. Asparagus is one of the first vegetables available in the Pacific Northwest in spring. That means the crates are available right about the time I start planting my springtime containers. The crates tend to be of pretty simple construction—compressed wood planks held together by loosely twisted wire. You need only to fill the space between the planks to make a planter box for cheap! Fill the gaps with Spanish moss or coconut fiber lining, and voilà!—you have a deep container for your plants. There are lots of everyday items that can act as planters. Here are just a few to inspire you.

COFFEE OR OLIVE OIL CANS: Some people still buy their coffee in metal cans; these make awesome containers for lettuces. Be sure to punch holes in the bottom of the can with a thick nail to allow for drainage. And plant just one lettuce per can! Olive oil cans follow the same guidelines. While these are not readily available to home cooks, ask at your local restaurant; they often buy olive oil in bulk, which comes in vibrant-colored tins.

FIVE-GALLON PLASTIC POTS: These are the sturdy plastic pots that shrubs and other large nursery plants often come in. Granted, they're not the most attractive pots you can find to grow food in, but they are free, and most retailers simply dispose of them. Check with your local plant nursery to see whether they have extras, and put a call out to gardening friends come spring. Chances are someone will have extra for you. Spray paint the exteriors a color that pops, and soon enough you'll have a patio full of eye-catching pots.

GUTTERS: Found on nearly every building and home, gutters are easy to come by. Their long, shallow shape is perfect for planting small lettuces. Be sure to drill drainage holes along the length of

the gutter before filling with potting soil and planting. Because gutter material is light (stainless steel, aluminum, or plastic), this is an ideal planter for hanging off a railing, and it uses the small space of a patio efficiently. You can pick up any length at a salvaged materials depot or a local construction site. Look for those made of stainless steel—they are the best looking.

PLASTIC MILK CRATES: Much like the asparagus crates, plastic milk crates make easy planters. You will need to fill in the gaps with either a liner (like a gently used plastic shower liner with drain holes), Spanish moss, or some sort of fiber—coconut fiber or even hay. I like to spray paint my milk crates white—this gives them a very clean, modern look.

WINE BOXES: If you live in or near wine country, wooden wine boxes shouldn't be too difficult to find. These shallow boxes are good for lettuces, seed starting, and microgreens. The best way to get your hands on them is by calling around to wineries and asking if they have extra. The thin wood on these boxes will last longer if you apply a coat of oil before planting; this helps give them a tough and slightly waterproof finish. Choose a Danish oil or orange oil from your local hardware store.

BURLAP, POTTING SOIL BAGS, AND OTHER SACKS: It is quite the hack, but you can grow plants directly in a bag of potting soil. This process will work, but it does not make the most attractive container. If you are dying to give it a try, go for it. You need only to steady the bag and split a hole in the top, then add your starts or seeds.

For a plant-in-a-bag project, I prefer a better-looking bag. Burlap sacks and plastic woven feed bags are a bit more shabby-chic. If you live in an area with local coffee-roasting companies, you should be able to find used burlap bags for free. Check in with your local roaster early in the season or during winter for a guaranteed source. Country feed stores are a good source for old feed bags. These often have the added benefit of vintage-looking logos—a great way to add character to your urban garden. Of course, fabric grow-bags made of synthetic woven fabrics are now widely available. These make for great, mobile containers—you can empty them in autumn and fold them up, storing them until next spring.

To plant in bags, simply fill with potting soil. Plant starts or seeds directly on the soil surface and be sure the edges of the bag don't come up around the plant to block out sunlight. This is a great way to plant potatoes, as you can add soil depth as they grow. (See Potatoes, page 43.) Soil kept in burlap will dry out quickly, so be sure to monitor water needs closely. The plastic feed bags will hang onto water as a plastic pot would, so be certain not to overwater these.

A final note—soil bags, burlap bags, and even the stronger feed bags break down over time, so they are probably a single-year kind of container. Be careful they don't get too threadbare, or the soil will spill out the bottom.

SOIL

The matter of soil may seem pretty obvious. You can grab any ol' bag of potting soil and grow something in it. But all potting soils are not created equal. Potting soil mix should drain well while still holding moisture. Most soil mixes are also formulated to maintain a certain level of lightness so that plants are able to breathe. Air is right up there with sunlight and water in importance to healthy, thriving plants.

Your potting soil should include a mix of compost or bark. These add richness and texture to the soil and will help to retain moisture. I recommend steering clear of any soil mixes containing peat or peat moss. Peat is not a sustainable resource, as it takes thousands of years to grow. Although peat does a good job of establishing a good growing environment, there are other, more sustainable and natural products to look for. Coconut fiber is a great example. The porous fibers of the coconut hair absorb and hang on to water and also let air circulate through the soil.

Don't pay too much attention to all the marketing claims on some potting soil. "Slow release of water to roots" and all sorts of other grand claims are merely attempts to get you to buy a product. Look for organic potting soil mixes from smaller regional companies rather than the national brands you'll find in big-box stores.

Choose a potting soil that has no added fertilizer or nutrients. It is best to add those on your own as needed for the particular plants you will grow.

It is a good idea to mix a few handfuls of organic compost into the soil in each pot. You can do this when you first plant, or add a top-dressing of compost around the base of your plants as the potting soil settles. Plan to top-dress each container a couple of times a season. It will help the soil hold on to moisture, which in turn will attract microorganisms. You'll find more information on keeping your soil in tip-top condition in the Feeding and Watering Plants chapter (page 91).

Once you have your plants started in a nice soil mix in your pots and are fertilizing at regular intervals, you can relax and let the plants do their thing. Each spring, however, it's a good idea to refresh the soil mix in any pots with dead plants. Perennial plants that have been in the same pot for years will also benefit from fresh soil. I will often add fresh potting soil to older plants if the existing soil has become really dry and caked over time.

To do this, tip out the entire plant and free up any root balls that have formed. I work directly on my deck and keep a dishpan and brush close by for sweeping up any soil that gets away. Break up and loosen the root ball with your fingers to free up the soil and roots. Then scoop in enough fresh potting mix to cover the bottom of the container so that the base of the plant stem is level with the container rim. Set in the plant and fill in the pot with fresh potting mix, holding the plant straight and firming the mix around the roots to stabilize it. Then water well. If the plant is severely root-bound, you may also loosen the roots as noted and transplant to a larger container.

Transplanting to a larger container will allow the plant to grow and thereby increase your overall harvest. You have to decide if transplanting is the best option for you. Want more production? Then the plant will need more space. If it produced the perfect amount of harvestable plant, you may use the same container.

When adding new plants to previously used containers, do not rely on simply digging a small hole in the soil and stuffing in a plant start. Old soils often contain dead roots from previous plants. Those roots will impede the new plant's roots and constrict air as the new plant tries to grow into the same small space. For that reason, just as in a field or on a farm, it's best to rework the soil before planting. Till the soil using a fork or your hands. Loosen it up, remove the root hairs, then gently work in some compost and a handful of fertilizer before adding a new plant start.

SUPPLIES

The basics just described are all you absolutely need to grow food at home. Because you are working in a controlled environment by planting in containers, you can get away with far fewer tools and supplies than if you were growing food in a garden plot. However, there are many gardening tools and devices that can expand the possibilities of any gardening adventure.

When you have a small apartment garden focused on growing food in containers, a big ol' garden rake is not going to be useful to you. In a small-scale garden environment, you need small-scale tools. Rather than investing money in a trowel or spade, you can perform the same tasks with simple kitchen items: one fork, one spoon, and one measuring cup.

Fork

Forks are great for digging in fertilizer and compost. Sprinkle some fertilizer or compost on the top of the soil, around the base of the plant. Use your fork to dig it into the first few inches of potting soil. Forks can also be used to lightly mix in seeds when sowing directly into a pot. Flower and looseleaf lettuce seeds can be sprinkled directly onto the potting soil surface. Using your fork, lightly pick over them and turn the soil gently. This light forking works well for small seeds that need only to be surface sown.

Spoon

A spoon is an obvious substitute for a shovel or trowel. When you are working with pots of soil, you don't need to do much digging. At most, you will need to dig down a few inches in the outer edges of the pot to check for moisture levels. To do this, rather than using a spade (which would actually displace too much soil), choose a soup spoon. The narrow handle is perfect for digging down deeply without disturbing the roots of the plant. In containers, root systems tend to press up against container walls and weave themselves in spirals at the bottom of the pot. You don't want to do too much damage to them, and a rounded spoon is soft enough that it won't invade the roots' space. Spoons are also great for removing moss-covered soil from pots. After winter, when the soil in some pots may be covered with dewy green moss, use the spoon as a skimmer to remove it. Replace the soil with fresh compost. I also use spoons to scoop out cigarette butts that visitors to my little garden can't seem to resist putting out in my plants! I spoon out about an inch of soil around each cig. Necessary? Probably not. But it makes me feel better, and I like to freshen up the soil now and again anyway.

Measuring Cup

A measuring cup does the job that a shovel or trowel would do in a backyard garden. Because you are adding only small amounts of potting soil to plants, the measuring cup allows for greater precision and also prevents too much soil from being dusted all over your patio as you work. Use a large measuring cup to scoop up and fill in potting soil for plants. When potting a new plant start, pour a few inches of potting soil into the pot, then add your start. Use the measuring cup to lightly sprinkle soil around the sides of the plant start until the pot is filled.

Garden Gloves

A pair of lightweight gloves will protect your hands and nails from soil and rough plant materials and spare them from the drying effects of frequent washing and scrubbing. Potting soil, although not as "muddy" as topsoil, will get under your nails and into your pores, and it's hard to scrub out. There are many glove choices, but an inexpensive pair of lightweight canvas gloves will suffice for a small urban garden.

Floating Row Cover

Floating row cover is a thin sheet of spun polyester that can be used in several ways. You can lay the cloth directly over seeds and plants for protection and insulation. In the early spring and late fall, row cover helps warm up the soil. It is also a good protector against garden pests. Pests like slugs and aphids are not typically a problem for apartment gardeners, but they have shown up on my deck on occasion—and I live three floors off the ground! Birds and other wildlife may sometimes visit your pots and toss the dirt around while looking for food. Floating row cover deters them from rooting around in your plants. In the heat of the summer, if you have full sun exposure, you may need to provide your plants with shade. Or maybe you need to insulate heat-loving plants. (See Tomato Care, page 48.) Stretching this cloth either over your pots like a tent or as a screen across your entire patio will help keep plants cool. Think of it as a protective umbrella for your plants.

Trellis

A structured trellis will offer support to any climbing or tall plants and is perfect for maximizing and managing your space. Cucumbers, peas, and nasturtiums are great for training up a trellis. Also, plants growing up a trellis offer subtle and lush privacy between neighbors in apartments or condos. Even if plants die back, a trellis is an excellent addition to the garden design as a vertical element, so be sure to choose a sturdy and attractive trellis structure that you won't mind looking at once winter arrives and the trellis is left bare.

Bamboo

Bamboo is like the duct tape of gardening—it has many uses. Use single stakes to support heavy plants, assemble a trellis, or form a teepee by tying twine or wire at the top. You can also easily build a shade wall for blocking out the strong summer sun—wrap floating row cover between two bamboo stakes and secure. Keep a few bamboo stakes of different lengths around. Most hardware stores sell six-foot lengths of sturdy bamboo that you can cut to any desired length with a handsaw. Bamboo is also available in shorter, thinner stakes that are more flexible and will not require cutting.

Potting Table

I have always wanted a potting table. You can work directly on the floor of your deck or patio; this is a fine and functional option. But a potting table frees up some space and will help keep things organized. These hip-height wonders are the perfect place to turn out soil, store extra pots, and shelve or hang equipment and supplies. If you have the space and budget for a potting table, I highly recommend getting one.

What to Grow for a Plentiful Harvest

Growing plants in containers is a tricky thing. There are plenty of resources available about growing food in containers that imply that this process is simple and straightforward—but most of us will find that it takes some trial and error.

My own experience is probably somewhat typical of what you can expect. Over the years, I've tried a mix of plants in a mix of containers and finally settled into a routine of what I grow. I steer clear of plants that won't produce much in a container or that have too long of a growing season. I find it best to focus on plants that are either very versatile in their culinary uses or will produce a generous harvest in a short amount of time. I use my apartment garden as creative inspiration for my meals, so I like to keep a little bit of a lot of different things.

Again, growing plants in a small space inhibits their growth potential. To understand why, it is helpful to understand the root systems of plants. This knowledge is of practical importance for gardeners—even novice gardeners who are just dabbling with growing food at home. As you begin to grasp basic growing concepts, it is much easier to make educated guesses on how best to grow successfully in your apartment garden. You don't need to get super science-y about it, but it is quite helpful to know just what is happening underneath the surface of your soil.

When a seed is first planted, a root is formed and begins to grow downward, sending out what is known as the *taproot*. This taproot will typically extend deep into the soil; it forms the beginnings of a plant's main root stem, from which smaller roots form and branch outward. These *root hairs* are like our own capillaries, fanning out horizontally and sometimes downward from the main root. Root hairs grow at various depths along the root system. Some branch out and spread wide just under the surface; others may form and branch out deeper in the subsoil.

This basic root system—encompassing the main root stem and its branch-like root hairs—has some very basic and obvious functions: absorbing nutrients and water for the plant. This happens most often in deep soil. The taproot is responsible for taking up nutrients. If you've ever transplanted a tree or shrub, you may have seen instructions to add fertilizer to the freshly dug hole. This is why. The deeper the fertilizer, the more readily available it is as food for the plant. Roots then store both nutrients and water to feed the plant. (The Feeding and Watering Plants chapter on page 91 has all the information needed to make sure plants are getting the proper nutrition for healthy growth.)

Without a strong root system, it is nearly impossible for any plant to grow to maturity. Sometimes, although we may interrupt the natural process of a plant life cycle, we are still able to harvest. For example, romaine lettuce grown in a shallow container may not grow to a full-sized leaf, but it will still grow and be plentiful. It is a delicate balance between giving the plant enough space to produce and making certain there is enough to harvest.

The following suggestions on what to grow in your apartment garden are based on plants that will do best in the sorts of pots and containers available at nurseries and retail shops. They also include plants I get asked about all the time and that seem to be universally popular—I'm lookin' at you, basil. There are plenty more plants that will do well in large, deep containers, but for an urban garden, I am assuming that the space you have to grow in is quite small. Additionally, these suggestions are based on plants that I have found to be great producers. You will be able to grow and harvest from these plants multiple times, particularly in the case of large fruiting plants like apple trees and blackberry canes. I have intentionally excluded plants that will produce in mediocre proportions, as well as plants that aren't guaranteed to be delicious. Things like parsley or cilantro aren't on the list because we can buy them with ease at most grocery stores nationwide— they're affordable and available year round. It is also good to note that I'm defining a "good producer" as a plant that will serve you several times.

With that, the following are some of my apartment favorites.

VEGETABLES

Vegetables are essentially the "meat and potatoes" of an apartment garden. These plants will add sustenance to your table and help make a meal. When the cupboards are bare, you should be able to rely on the garden to come through and provide some key fresh ingredients that will inspire a meal.

Vegetable plants have higher nutrient needs than herb and flower plants, so you will have to be mindful of fertilizing.

I recommend keeping some sort of log so you know when to fertilize again. (I do this by creating an appointment in my online calendar every six weeks or so.) Different plants, too, have varying requirements—but will need some combination of nitrogen, phosphorus, and potassium: NPK. Leafy greens need plenty of nitrogen (N), as nitrogen supports leafy green growth in all plants. Fruiting plants grown for their fruits (like peas or cucumbers) rather than for their leaves or roots require more phosphorus (P). Potassium (K) is needed in small amounts by all kinds of plants for strong and consistent root growth and overall plant health. As plants have individual requirements, I buy my fertilizer components in bulk and tailor the proportions specifically to each pot. You can read more about how to properly feed your plants in the Feeding and Watering Plants chapter, page 91.

You need to be especially mindful about watering your vegetable plants. If you stress the plant by under- or overwatering, odds are it won't produce as expected. Although herbs will bounce back from neglect over time, with vegetables you run the risk of damaging the plant beyond repair.

Harvesting from your plants is one of the single most important things you can do. A plant's life cycle is such that it grows to maturity and sets seed so that future generations can live on. By interrupting this process (halting its ability to make seeds by harvesting) you ensure that the plant will continue the cycle a little bit longer. In a funny way, you are making the plant stress that it will not survive. Plants are genetically disposed to keep striving to produce offspring so that a new generation can live on. Essentially, interrupting this process equals higher yields.

The following list of fruits and vegetables to grow in an apartment garden is not utterly inclusive, but it is a solid guide for both beginners and people who really want to produce as much as they can in a small amount of space. These plants were chosen for one or more of several key characteristics—ease, taste, or high yields—that make them worth growing.

Bitter Greens

Arugula is a spicy, bitter salad green. Dandelion greens are bitter—an excellent leaf that detoxes our systems. A member of the Brassicaceae or mustard family, arugula is considered a cold-weather crop and does well in the cooler temperatures of early spring and fall. (Most mustard leaves can be grown the same.) People often ask me why their arugula didn't do well; more often than not, it's because they waited too long to sow seeds and the weather was already too warm. Arugula and dandelion both produce long flat leaves with a distinct peppery/bitter flavor. Each seed produces one thin stem from which leaves grow. You can further your harvest by cutting them back often—leaves will regenerate once and maybe even twice before getting too spicy, woody, or bitter.

WHERE AND WHEN TO PLANT

Sow arugula or dandelion seeds in the top layer of potting soil in March or April. Sow again in late summer and early fall—late August and anytime through October.

POT SIZE

If given the room, arugula plants may grow to well over 2 feet tall. In a small to medium container, however, leaves grow to the perfect size for salad.

HOW TO HARVEST

Cut arugula and dandelion greens at the base of each leaf off the main stem. You can decide for yourself when the leaf is big enough. For a mellow, spicy flavor and a tender green, harvest when leaves are young—about 3 to 4 inches. If you prefer a stronger flavor and a thicker, crunchier stem, allow them to grow to 5 to 6 inches and cut the entire stem at its base. Arugula bolts (goes to flower) quickly in heat. If this happens, strip the woody stem of its leaves and use both the leaves and flowers in your salads. Woody stems can be chopped finely and used to make a *gremolata* (a chopped herb condiment) or as stuffing for savory dishes.

Cucumber

Cucumbers do well in containers because individual vines are prolific and will produce a decent amount of fruit even when given a small space. Growing in a large container will provide enough fruit to make any effort worthwhile. (Although ideally they should be grown in the ground, as their taproots will run down as far as two feet if given the chance.)

Choose small varieties, as they will mature fairly quickly. Cornichons, gherkins, and other pickling cucumbers do better in containers than the larger slicing varieties.

WHERE AND WHEN TO PLANT

Plant out cucumber seeds throughout June in the Pacific Northwest (earlier in warmer climates). They don't take super well to transplanting, but you can try starting them indoors in early May for a jump on the season.

POT SIZE

Use a large pot for cucumbers, and sow four seeds per pot at the farthest corners from each other. A cucumber's side roots, much like zucchini's, tend to branch out widely in just the first few inches of soil layer, so a wide square pot offers the best space. Thin out any small vines after six weeks to allow the more prolific vines space to grow.

HOW TO HARVEST

Snap cucumbers from the stem when they are ready, or use a flat knife to cut them off just above where the stem connects to the fruit. Small varieties are best harvested when they are just that— small. Don't try to grow them larger, as they turn bitter and the seed membrane becomes weblike and unpalatable.

Kale

Here is the most important thing to know and consider when planting kale in containers: its natural root system is deep, thick, and dense with root hairs. That means the more soil space you can give it to grow and stretch, the taller the plant will be and the more leaves it will produce for harvesting. Smaller pot equals smaller leaves—totally unsatisfying. Most people go for lacinato kale (a.k.a. dino kale, Tuscan kale), but these rules apply for all kale types—the shorter, frillier versions (Russian kales) as well as the tall, flat "Italian" kales.

WHERE AND WHEN TO PLANT

Kale is an exceptional plant thanks to its seasonal fortitude: it can be planted damn near all year long—through spring, summer, and autumn—and one plant will often span two or three seasons.

POT SIZE

Plant alone in a deep pot—at least 18 inches deep—and resist the urge to underplant. You can mulch the soil surface with moss, gravel, or organic mulch, but you don't want other root systems crowding the pot.

HOW TO HARVEST

Harvest leaves off the stem of the plant, starting at the bottom and working your way up. At a certain point, you will have a long, naked kale stalk with only green leaves on top—sort of like a mini-palm tree.

Lettuce

Whether you opt for butterhead, romaine, crisphead, or looseleaf, lettuce is one of the easiest plants to grow. Little Gem (a romaine variety), Rouge d'Hiver (a cross between romaine and butterhead), and Oak Leaf (a looseleaf lettuce) are all great choices. If you'd like a summer lettuce, be sure to choose a heat-tolerant variety. If you know you'll be planting in fall, a cool-season lettuce is in order. For flexibility, purchase a variety of lettuce seeds at the beginning of the year and sow according to the season.

WHERE AND WHEN TO PLANT

Lettuce can be sown almost any time of year, depending on your climate, so it's best to read the back of the seed packets to determine the timing that is best for each type.

POT SIZE

Sow seeds in a long, shallow, pale-colored plastic container, since lettuces are shallow-rooted, and plastic containers hold water a bit

longer than clay ones. Smaller pots tend to heat up faster than a large deep pot, so choosing a light color helps keep the roots cool, as well. Be sure to keep the seedbed moist until seeds germinate, which typically happens in five to seven days.

HOW TO HARVEST

To harvest lettuce, try to remove the larger outer leaves first. Using a small pair of scissors, cut the individual leaf stems as close to the base of the main stem as possible, leaving some interior leaves behind. These leaves will soon size up and become harvestable outer leaves; thus you're creating a cycle of lettuce leaves to harvest. If you prefer to harvest complete heads of lettuce, do so when the heads are full and the outer leaves are starting to yellow and wilt; just know that if you cut the entire plant, the odds of its regenerating are reduced.

Potatoes

Potatoes grow underground and are a "tuber"—a plant that is enlarged to store nutrients and has the ability to make a new plant. Potatoes, yams, and even dahlias are considered tubers. When planted in a field, it's called "hilling up" potatoes, as farmers will form hills of soil around the potato stem to maximize production— we need to mimic this process.

WHERE AND WHEN TO PLANT

To grow potatoes, cut off a small piece with an eye (often the eyes already have sprouts emerging) and bury it under about 3 inches of soil. Place in a sunny spot and keep watered. The plant will eventually send up a stem and leaves. Once these stems are about 4 inches tall, cover them with soil (always leaving a little bit of leaf showing) in order for the plant to produce more potatoes. Continue doing this as the stems grow taller—grow, cover with soil, grow, cover with soil. Note: sweet potatoes and potatoes are different plants, but can be grown in the same manner, though sweet potatoes will take longer—about three months.

Potatoes do not like superhot weather—for gardeners in the northern United States, spring is a great time to plant. For southern gardeners, you'll have to wait until the heat of summer begins to wane, or try putting your potato bags in a cool, shaded spot that gets only morning sun, such as a north-facing balcony.

POT SIZE

To create soil depth, potatoes can be grown in bags, garbage cans, and deep containers used exclusively for potatoes. Essentially, any container in which a potato plant can grow vertically, allowing you to cover their stems and roots, will work.

HOW TO HARVEST

After the plant flowers and once the leaves start dying back, it's time to harvest by digging up the potatoes! Reuse the soil and bag for another planting.

Snap Peas

Snap peas are one of the earliest seeds you can sow in the spring, especially if you're using a container, as you don't need to wait for the soil to dry up after winter rains. Peas have root systems that spread laterally but don't grow down too deep and are therefore great for containers. They also put up pretty sweet pea flowers (that then turn into peas) and grow tall, adding some height to the garden. In addition to pea pods, you can also harvest pea vines from the plant without hurting production too much. Clip new vine growth and use in sautés or soups.

WHERE AND WHEN TO PLANT

Sow pea seeds directly into your pot in early spring—from around the middle of March to the beginning of April—and cover with an inch of soil. Keep the seedbed well watered so the buried seeds stay moist until germination.

POT SIZE

Plant in a large, wide, deep pot. Choose the largest terra-cotta or plastic pot you can find. I categorize large pots as those about 18 inches deep and wide.

HOW TO HARVEST

Snap the peas from the vine when the pods are full and firm but still tender, and be sure to keep the plant harvested. If you leave mature pea pods on the vine, the plant will stop producing altogether (convinced that its work is done for the season), and the pea pods will become chewy and thick.

Tomatoes and Peppers

Tomatoes and peppers have similar growing habits, so I'm clumping them together.

WHERE AND WHEN TO PLANT

Plant tomatoes and peppers from mid-May through early June. Plant out tomato starts once evening temperatures are consistently above 60 degrees F. Choose a start that produces small- to medium-sized fruits. The larger the fruit produced, the

more space the plant will need to grow. (Remember, containers restrict plant growth, so the smaller the fruit, the more likely you will have success.) Most locations can plant out in mid- to late May. Bury some stem when you plant the start—tomatoes have aerial roots that will grow out from the stem, helping to anchor the plant.

POT SIZE

Use a large pot for tomatoes, and plant only one start per pot! Tomato and pepper root systems are deep and have a lot of root hairs that will fill the soil. You can underplant the soil around the tomato with basil seed or plants, which will not overcrowd the pot with roots. Tomatoes will eventually need support—a bamboo teepee is a perfect solution—tie the stem to the poles. Peppers also do well with only one plant per pot. Basically, leave 14 to 18 inches for each plant to grow—that's a typical diameter for a large pot. If growing in bigger containers, feel free to space out appropriately.

HOW TO HARVEST

Harvest tomatoes and peppers when the fruits have turned the desired/intended color and easily release from the vine with a gentle tug or twist. Fruits will continue to ripen on the counter after harvest, so if you harvest too early, just let them sit for a few days before eating.

Peppers All Year Long

Peppers can be treated as a perennial plant! Occasionally, when I have a really strong pepper plant that is a good producer, I'll bring it inside over winter, fertilize and prune it, and see if I can get it to flower and produce once more.

Tomato Care

Tomatoes do well with a bit of special attention during the growing season, particularly if you live in a maritime climate like mine in Seattle. Here are a few tips for tomato care.

- Water tomatoes in the morning; this gives the wet soil time to warm up during the day. Tomatoes, along with other nightshade plants, are sensitive to cold. Can you imagine sitting outside, overnight, wrapped in a wet blanket? That's cold!
- Consider installing a water wall or similar insulating, heat-radiating product around tomatoes. In my own garden, I often post four bamboo stakes around the pot and wrap it with a piece of floating row cover, which traps a bit of heat while allowing light to come through.
- Support tomato plants as they grow. In a backyard garden, I would never recommend a tomato cage because indeterminate tomatoes grow fast and often outgrow these, but in a container, a tomato cage works well. In my own garden, I build a simple teepee using three bamboo canes about 5 feet tall, then tie tomato stems to them while training them up.
- Just after midseason, when tomato plants have set fruit that is mostly still green and have a dense mass of leaves, I prune excess stems from the plant. Leaves are wonderful, as they take in sunlight and help to nourish plants, but they also block air flow and can shade fruit from the sun. If a plant is very dense, I prune out about 30 percent of leafy stems. Use your best judgment—the goal early on is to open up the plant, create airflow, and make sure all fruit is reached by sunlight.

- At the end of the growing season, when the days are shorter and the temperatures start to drop (toward the end of August in most regions), I prune off all growing tips with flowers and small green fruit from my tomato plants. Flowers will keep forming fruits, but it's too late for them to mature fully, and if a green fruit is too small (less than 70 percent of mature size), it will not ripen. To prune fruit and flowers from plants may seem counterintuitive, but you want them to focus *all* of their energy on producing seed—that is, ripening the fruit that has already formed.

Zucchini

Zucchini and other summer squashes are the plants that keep on giving. Squashes are prolific, and you don't need many to keep you in a productive crop most of the summer. Zucchini can be harvested when small or left alone to get big and fat. Just remember that the longer you leave the squash on a plant, the less the plant will produce, and the bigger the seeds and the seed membranes will become.

WHERE AND WHEN TO PLANT

For zucchini and summer squashes, follow the same rules as for cucumbers. (Squashes and cucumbers come from the same cucurbit plant family, so they have similar planting needs.) Sow zucchini seeds in early June or late May if the temperatures are consistently above 60 degrees F. You can also sow in late June or even early July for a late-season crop, but if it is a cool summer, fruit may not have time to mature.

POT SIZE

Use a large pot for zucchini, and sow three seeds, spacing them evenly. Zucchini roots spread out shallowly. They tend to be fat and fleshy down to about 7 or 8 inches, then fan out into root hairs. For this reason they are well suited to container growing. After about six weeks of growth, thin any vines that are being dwarfed.

HOW TO HARVEST

Snap zucchini straight from the stem, or cut them using a straight-edged knife. You can harvest zucchini when they are young or wait until they are older and riper. Younger squashes are quite firm and will hold their shape in sautés or on the grill. A more mature fruit

has a softer flesh and larger seeds. It is a personal preference for when it's best to harvest.

SWEET FRUITS

Apple Trees

Fruit trees are such a treat to grow on an outdoor patio or balcony. New cultivars—columnar apple trees—grow from a single trunk that produces short branches. These are perfect for anyone with a limited amount of space. You can also seek out a "mini-dwarf" tree, which should get no more than 8 feet tall. Apple trees do get tall, even in pots, so choose wisely if you'd like them to produce. Most apple trees also need another tree for pollination (unless they are self-pollinating) so plan to grow two trees side by side.

WHERE AND WHEN TO PLANT

To produce healthy fruit, fruiting plants need a lot of direct sunlight. Apple trees require at least six to eight hours of direct sunlight. Plant bare root trees when temperatures are cooler—sometime between autumn and spring.

POT SIZE

To grow an apple tree in a pot, you need a container size of at least 25 gallons—the larger the container, the larger the tree. I recommend putting the pot up on casters before filling it with soil and planting. This allows you to move the tree around with ease.

Pollination

To put it simply, pollination leads to the production of fruits we eat. Fruits we eat contain seeds to create more plants. It's the circle of life. Flowers are either male or female. A male flower produces pollen on a stamen (technically, on the anther on a stamen) and then as pollen is moved from male plant to female, pollination occurs. Pollination happens thanks to wind, water, insects, and birds, and that's why we often hear so much about attracting good pollinators to the garden!

As urban container gardeners, we don't need to super actively concentrate on pollinators. If you grow a collection of plants throughout seasons and have several plant families, the odds are high that you'll attract pollinators to your garden. That said, it is valuable to understand the process in the event your garden has poor pollination. If you have a squash vine or apple tree full of flowers, but no fruit forms, pollination may be the missing link. You can manually pollinate, using a cotton swab to move pollen from male plants to female, or you can be sure to plant some flowers that attract the good pollinators, like hyssop, thymes, and mints.

HOW TO HARVEST

Apples are harvested just like any other fruit—when fruits come off easily with a gentle pull or twist, they are ready to eat.

Blueberries/Blackberry Bushes

There are new cultivars of berries introduced every season that are purposely bred to do well in containers. I love the Apache blackberry "tree"—a tall, thornless bush that produces exceptional blackberries. There are several varieties that are bred to be about 3 feet tall.

WHERE AND WHEN TO PLANT
Choose a spot that receives at least eight full hours of direct sunlight during the summer months. Plant with potting soil—do not use soil from the ground, which will be too heavy and choke the root system. Plant all berries as starts in early spring.

POT SIZE
Choose a large pot for one plant—you will need at least 20 gallons of soil to start. Blackberries will need to be moved into bigger pots year after year—this helps to establish a strong root system. Blackberries need support—I prefer a latticework trellis, whether made from wood or metal. Blueberries can be planted in slightly smaller pots—one plant for every 20-gallon container.

HOW TO HARVEST
Harvest berries in late summer, when fruits are full and juicy. Harvest on a dry day, not after rain or just after watering, as the plant takes up water quickly and this results in watery-tasting fruit! When they are ripe and ready, berries fall off easily into your hand.

Strawberries
Strawberries are fun to grow because a single plant can tolerate the confinement of a small pot, and they are pretty plants as well. They are one of the first plants to come up in spring, and when the weather really warms up, small fruits form to announce summer's arrival. If you hope to harvest bowl after bowl of strawberries, you should really try to find a big patch to grow them in. But if you

don't mind a small bowlful every year, and you're in it just for the thrill, a plant or two will do.

WHERE AND WHEN TO PLANT

Strawberries can be set out first thing in spring. Purchase starts rather than trying to grow from seed, or (if you have access to a strawberry patch) clip a runner and plant that. In fall, be sure to mulch the pot completely so the plants are protected and will survive the winter. I've had the same strawberry plants for four years now and don't invest much time in them other than watering and mulching.

POT SIZE

One strawberry plant will fit in a small pot that is at least 6 inches deep. In a good year with hot weather, you'll harvest four or five strawberries from the plant. If you'd like more, try starting with one plant in a long narrow pot. The plant will send out runners that will eventually grow into full plants.

HOW TO HARVEST

You know how to harvest strawberries! Just pick them off the stem. When they are ripe and ready, they will fall off easily into your hand.

HERBS

Herbs are champions in the apartment garden: no matter how much you harvest, they keep on giving. Herbs are fairly easy to grow, though they require varying pot sizes depending on their root systems. Many herbs are perennials, so they return year after

OREGANO

FLAT-LEAF PARSLEY

THYME

CHIVES

ROSEMARY

SAGE

MINT

year, signaling spring's arrival. You can overwinter perennial herbs in their pots. Most will come back in spring even when neglected over the winter—a great choice for the lazy gardener.

Herbs are potent little plants, and your kitchen will never feel lacking with bunches of fresh stems and branches on hand. Herbs may be dried or infused to extend their life outside of the garden. For the apartment garden, herbs are the quintessential low-maintenance, high-reward plants to grow.

Anise Hyssop

The unique flavor of anise hyssop is part licorice, part mint, a little bit like honey—herbal perfection. It is nice addition to grain salads and as a digestive tea or tisane after a big meal or between courses. This herb is best grown from seed. Recently, I've seen anise hyssop starts at the nursery, but don't count on finding them easily. The plant grows tall, sturdy stalks topped with vibrant purple flowers. Anise hyssop is a perennial and will come back year after year.

WHERE AND WHEN TO PLANT

Anise hyssop can be sown in spring, directly in a pot. The seeds are super tiny and need only to be pressed into the soil. Because the seeds are so light and small, anise hyssop tends to spread seed liberally after it flowers. Expect it to crop up in other pots the following year. I let these stray seeds grow to small seedlings before I repot them or give them away to friends. Anise hyssop likes sun but will do well in partial shade with at least six to eight hours of sunlight.

POT SIZE

Anise hyssop appreciates some room to grow, so select a deep pot. Flower stalks may reach over 2 feet tall, and the extra depth helps the plant to grow high. Shoot for a 2-foot depth and about that much width on a pot.

HOW TO HARVEST

Cut off an entire stalk just above a leaf line. When the plant flowers, cut back the entire main stem, as it may regenerate growth.

Perennial Herbs

Perennials are plants that live for longer than two years in succession. For apartment and container gardens focused on edibles, this mostly applies to herbaceous plants. These plants grow in spring, flower in summer, and go dormant in winter. The following year they put on growth again from the same rootstock, and some perennial plants, like anise hyssop, also distribute seed as annuals do. For this reason, perennials can often be divided and shared with fellow gardeners.

Perennials are easy to keep in an apartment garden, as they generally need less attention than annuals do and are fairly hardy. In temperate climates, like in the Pacific Northwest, most perennials will survive outside over winter, even without extra mulching. An added benefit, as small apartments typically don't have extra room to bring all those pots indoors! If you live in a region with hard frosts, it is best to move your perennials under some form of protection. A cellar or unheated garage will work

Basil

Basil is a warm-weather crop, sensitive to the cold, so you have to time it just right in order for basil to succeed. Wait to plant seeds or starts until temperatures are consistently above 60 degrees F at night—basil will go black and rot when night temperatures drop too low.

WHERE AND WHEN TO PLANT

Basil can be planted out with tomatoes when the weather is consistently warm. I typically underplant (plant one plant under another) tomatoes with basil starts. If you're using a start from

well. For any pots left outdoors, plan to insulate the soil with a thick layer of mulch, then wait the winter out and hope for the best. On my own patio, there have been really cold years in which I've lost geraniums, lovage, and scented sages, but they are easily replaced come spring.

When planting for the first time, be sure to give perennial plants plenty of space to stretch their roots and grow, as you will have them in your garden for longer than a year. The bigger the pot, the more plant matter you'll have to harvest, so select your favorites and give them some room to grow.

The following is a quick list of perennial herbs to consider when you're starting your apartment garden.

- Chives
- Dill
- Lemon balm
- Lovage
- Mint
- Oregano
- Rosemary
- Sage
- Thyme

the nursery, be sure to divide the clump into individual plants and leave at least 6 inches between them. Seeds can't be sown outdoors until weather warms up, so planting a start will speed up harvest. Plant both seeds and a start simultaneously, which will keep you in basil through summer and into fall.

POT SIZE

Choose a medium-sized pot with good drainage—basil does *not* like wet feet at night. Basil needs room to grow, so be sure to plant in a pot that is at least 12 inches deep.

HOW TO HARVEST

Basil is best when you pinch it back to extend the growing cycle. To pinch back use your fingertips or scissors to cut the stem just above the next lower set of leaves, or an even lower set of leaves if the stem is tall. In my gardens, I pinch off at varying heights because pinching off will force the plant to branch out. Two stems will form where there was once one (a very common response for many plants), so the plant will become bushy. By varying the lengths at which you pinch off, you'll wind up with a good-looking, well-rounded bushy plant. If you do not pinch off, basil plants will go to seed at the height of summer, flowering and losing its flavorful potency. To harvest whole stems, cut the entire stem from the plant, making sure to cut just above the first set of leaves—do not pluck leaves from stems!

Chervil

Chervil is one of my very favorite herbs. With tender fernlike leaves, it is extremely dainty and delicate. The flavor is not unlike dill, but it is sharper and more crisp. It doesn't linger on your

Herbs for Shade

Not every patio, balcony, or deck gets enough sun to support growing food at home. But there is still hope for such spaces, although some plants won't grow as vigorously as they would in full sun. The following plants can tolerate some shade:

- Angelica
- Anise hyssop
- Bay
- Chervil
- Lemon balm
- Mint
- Parsley
- Sweet cicely
- Sweet woodruff

palate as dill can, and it won't overpower a dish. Chervil is a great match for eggs, light broths, and white fish of any kind.

WHERE AND WHEN TO PLANT

Chervil can be sown from seed in early spring well before many other plants or in late summer for a second crop. Depending on the zone, plants sown in February or March often flower and reseed themselves when the temperatures are just right. Chervil does well in partial shade; in fact, if it gets too warm, it will bolt quickly.

POT SIZE

Chervil can be grown in a medium-depth pot, 8 to 12 inches deep. The wider the pot, the more the plant will fill in, so keep that in mind when choosing.

HOW TO HARVEST

Cut the entire stem of chervil and use both leaves and stem. The plant will quickly fill back in.

Chives

Chives do well in containers, look beautiful, are quite flavorful, and come back year after year. This plant sends up thin hollow stalks tasting strongly of onion. When chives blossom (typically in late May or early June), the flower heads are equally flavorful and can be used in salads and dressings of any kind. After flowering, cut back the entire plant to about 1 inch; it will grow and flower again later in summer.

WHERE AND WHEN TO PLANT

Chives can be sown from seed early in April. They are prolific and grow quickly, so I recommend purchasing seeds instead of starts, or taking a small clump from a friend's garden. Chives will readily reseed if given the opportunity, so be diligent about deadheading the spent blossoms, which contain the seed.

POT SIZE

A medium-sized pot is usually plenty for a steady supply of chives from spring through summer. Pick a pot that is at least 12 inches deep and about that wide.

HOW TO HARVEST

Cut chive stems close to the base of the plant, leaving about an inch of green. The plant will fill back in. Start from the outside of the plant and work your way in as new growth develops. When the plant flowers, pick off the entire flower head and crumble to separate the purple blossoms to use in recipes.

Lemon Verbena

Growing lemon verbena is not entirely practical for the apartment gardener; because it is a tender perennial, you have to closely monitor its condition, taking it indoors to overwinter. But with that extra effort comes a handsome reward. Lemon verbena is a beautiful plant to grow, with slender, twig-like branches and long, rippled, glossy leaves that are delicate and stunning. There is truly nothing like lemon verbena—its flavor is both floral and lemony. Try lemon verbena in beverages and infused into sugar. It also makes an interesting addition (in small amounts) to a green salad and is fabulous when mashed up into a *gremolata* to accompany lamb.

WHERE AND WHEN TO PLANT

Purchase a start for lemon verbena in late spring—no earlier than May. Verbena likes hot conditions, so it's best to set the plant in full sun and be sure to keep it watered regularly.

POT SIZE

A large pot will allow for a large shrub with many branches and leaves. Choose a container at least 2 feet deep and about as wide so the lemon verbena can grow big and tall.

HOW TO HARVEST

Cut off entire branches from the plant; steer clear of the main stem and cut just above a set of leaves. It will regrow.

Lovage

Lovage looks and tastes like celery with a more pronounced flavor. The leaves are a bit bigger and can be chopped into salads, soups, and seafood dishes. Lovage is a perennial that will come back year after year and can withstand some neglect. I stuck some lovage root in a pot many years ago, and except for some watering and pruning back in fall, I haven't done a thing to help it along. Lovage may flower and seed if you give it enough room to grow. I keep lovage in a medium-sized pot, and it has flowered only occasionally. On bigger plants, you can collect the seed in late summer and used it to stock your pantry. Ground up, the seed can be used as a spice rub on meat or fish, or even as an addition to cinnamon in fruit pies and crisps.

WHERE AND WHEN TO PLANT

Lovage can be planted from rootstock in fall—ask a friend to cut you a small portion. Place in a large pot of soil, water, and mulch with dry leaves for insulation over the winter. If you don't have a cutting, in early spring purchase a start and plant it directly into your pot.

POT SIZE

With this herb, the bigger the pot, the bigger the plant. A medium- to large-sized pot about 1 foot deep and about as wide will produce enough to use occasionally throughout the year. If you have the space for a larger pot, though, I highly recommend it. This plant will grow very tall and wide if you let it, and it's an absolute marvel to see in a garden.

HOW TO HARVEST

Cut lovage at the base of the stems, working from the outside of the plant in. Big outer stems can often be quite strong in flavor, so make sure to harvest smaller tender stalks often. The plant will continue to produce through summer.

Marjoram

Marjoram is a strong-flavored herb, very similar to oregano but with a softer note. It can be added raw to dishes but will also withstand some heat from cooking. Try it in tomato sauces and gravies or as a small addition to salads. Marjoram is a perennial herb, though it can be tender, and you will often see it sold as an annual. It's a great herb for drying.

WHERE AND WHEN TO PLANT

Sow marjoram seeds directly into pots in April, or purchase a start and plant out. Better yet, start seeds inside in March. They grow quickly and will take off once it's warm enough to set them outside in late spring.

POT SIZE

A medium-sized pot will suffice for marjoram. Pick a pot a bit deeper than 6 inches with a wide opening.

HOW TO HARVEST

You can harvest whole stems of marjoram by cutting at the base of the stem. Once the plant flowers, cut back about halfway and it will put on new growth quickly.

Mint

Mint is a fabulous herb to perk up salads, crush into a pesto for roasted meats, or add to a fizzy summertime beverage. Mint is a considered a "runner"—a plant that sends out horizontal root runners that produce new stalks. Choose a long, shallow pot to allow it room to spread. Most garden centers carry starts of mint, or you can ask a neighbor for a clipping. Mint is prolific and will establish itself quickly. It is also a great herb to dry and save for tisanes.

WHERE AND WHEN TO PLANT

Mint can be planted out nearly all year long. Plant mint starts in the spring through early summer or fall in most areas. Plant in full to partial sun and keep the soil moist. However, mint does not like wet feet, so be mindful that the soil drains well and do not let water stand in the drainage saucer after watering.

POT SIZE

For a continuous supply of mint, choose a medium-sized pot, at least 10 inches deep and 9 inches wide.

HOW TO HARVEST

Cut entire stems from the mint plant, at their base, as close to the soil as possible.

Thyme

Thyme is one of the most versatile herbs to cook with. It is easy to grow and will come back year after year. Thyme is indispensable in stocks or for roasting meats, but it can also be used in sweet desserts and pairs well with fruit such as plums and blueberries. Be sure to select a culinary thyme (English thyme is a favorite), as there are many members in the thyme family and not all of them taste great. If you purchase a start, taste a leaf first to see if you like the flavor. Scented thymes are interesting additions to the garden. Lemon thyme has a distinctive citrus aroma and can be used in most recipes that call for English thyme.

WHERE AND WHEN TO PLANT

Thyme is a hardy herb, adaptable to various weather conditions. You can plant starts in spring, summer, or fall with good results. Thyme does well in dappled shade and does not need full sun to be vigorous.

POT SIZE

Thyme has a shallow root system but will spread if you give it space to branch out. Grow thyme in a wide, shallow pot or even a wooden flat or box.

HOW TO HARVEST

Choose whole branches of thyme and cut them at the base, just above a set of leaves. You should also cut back your thyme in early summer after it blooms (generally in June), as it will then fill in and provide tender bushy growth all summer and through fall.

FLOWERS

Flowers are a beautiful addition to any garden. Thin stems swaying in the breeze topped with bright-colored blossoms add life and texture to the garden. Not only are flowers visually stunning, but they also attract pollinators. Bees, other insects, and hummingbirds fly from plant to plant, eating nectar and spreading pollen. This cross-pollination is crucial for some plants to fruit or flower, so flowers are an important part of a healthy garden ecosystem. Luckily, some flowers play a role in our kitchens as well. Petals are often edible—though few have a distinctive flavor, they add eye appeal with their delicate forms and colors—and some leaves of flowering plants can be used in salads and cocktails. Many plants also produce edible seeds that can be used as garnish on dishes or dried and kept for winter pantry-stocking. Get creative and use blossoms in teas and infusions, try chopping stems into salads, or use leaves as part of your table setting.

Many flowers will reseed themselves if given the opportunity, so be prepared to either deadhead plants (remove all the dead, dry flower heads that hold the seeds) and save the seed, or allow them to spread among your containers. It's pretty cool to let flowers drop seed and see where they crop up the following year. I have grown anise hyssop in one pot, only to have new anise hyssop plants sprout up across the deck in a pot 10 feet away the following year. It's pretty amazing that a little seed can travel so far, land on a small surface of soil, survive the winter, and create a new plant.

Borage

These tall, prickly-stemmed plants are not only a gorgeous addition to a small garden, but also a tasty one. Borage grows 2 to 3 feet tall on a sturdy stalk that sends out sparse but large, hairy, edible leaves. Harvest young leaves for the best flavor—the spiky hairs on mature leaves can turn some people off. The leaves have a slight cucumber flavor, great for a Pimm's Cup cocktail. Flowers blossom in a deep purple-blue and can be used as an edible garnish. This plant attracts pollinators to the garden and is therefore a great plant to grow alongside fruiting vegetables.

WHERE AND WHEN TO PLANT

Plant borage seeds in late spring or early summer, sometime between May and June, as this plant needs warmer soil temperatures to germinate.

POT SIZE

Plant borage in a deep pot. When given plenty of space for the roots to branch out, the plant can grow to maturity, which is when it is most stunning. Sow four to six seeds directly into the potting soil; if all germinate, you will need to thin them, leaving the two or three strongest seedlings in the container.

HOW TO HARVEST

Harvest borage leaves by pulling or clipping new small leaves from the main stem. Harvest borage flowers when the petals fully open and turn deep blue.

Chamomile

Chamomile is a wispy-stemmed plant with small, white, daisy-like flowers. The plants have a distinctive sweet-floral scent, and flower buds can be used in teas or sweet recipes. This plant is medicinal and both calms nerves and aids in digestion. Chamomile comes in many varieties, but the self-seeding annual German chamomile is the common plant for teas and infusions.

WHERE AND WHEN TO PLANT

Chamomile prefers full sun and should be planted in late spring, once temperatures have warmed and remain consistent. Because chamomile has such delicate stems, it makes for a great border plant. Try planting a start close to the container's edge, and allow the stems to droop over. One chamomile start would fit nicely in a large container planted with borage.

POT SIZE

German chamomile, with its shallow root system, grows low to the ground and spreads. Try tucking this plant into a small pot—6 inches deep and at least that wide at the rim. The larger the pot, the larger the harvest will be.

HOW TO HARVEST

Pop full flower heads off the plant for use in recipes. You can use them fresh or place them in a single layer on a drying rack. Once dry, they can be stored in a small spice jar in your pantry.

Nigella

Nigella is more commonly known as love-in-a-mist, and several plant species go by the name. For culinary use, choose *Nigella sativa*, also known as black cumin or onion seed. Cornflower blue, sharply triangular flowers bloom on a thin stem with wispy fronds that look like fennel. Once the blooms fade, thin-skinned seedpods develop—they look like paper lanterns. Some people use the dried pods in floral arrangements, but the seeds are edible and can be used as garnish, just like poppy seeds.

WHERE AND WHEN TO PLANT

Direct-sow nigella seeds in spring, with successive sowings through early summer. This plant likes sun but does not need constant exposure. A pot with morning sun works well. Nigella is a self-seeding annual.

POT SIZE

For a splash of color and good production of seeds, give nigella lots of room to grow. Choose a deep pot—at least eighteen inches. The width of the pot is not as important, as nigella grows tall and the roots do not spread wide.

HOW TO HARVEST

Leave the flowers to form seedpods. When the seedpods have dried and turned brown, pull off the heads and shake out the seeds. Store the seeds in a glass spice container in your spice cupboard.

Scented Geraniums

Scented geraniums come in varying hues of green or have variegated leaves, which are heavily perfumed and can be harvested to use in sweet recipes. Geraniums come back each year (unless it's a really cold winter with several freezes) and will survive warm weather with blatant neglect. Many flower in varying shades of pink and white, but it's the foliage that holds the oil. To decide which geranium to purchase, rub a leaf gently between your thumb and index finger to pick up some of the plant's natural oil, then smell it to see whether you like the scent. Scented geraniums come in a wide range of aromas—mint, nutmeg, rose, lemon, and many others—rose geranium is my fave.

WHERE AND WHEN TO PLANT

Geraniums do well in dappled sun or partly shady spaces, so long as they get some sunlight. They can be planted nearly any time of the year. If you have winters with long freezes, move the plants inside until spring.

POT SIZE

You can use smaller pots for geraniums, as you likely won't use much in recipes. A few leaves a year will keep you well stocked. Choose a pot at least 8 inches deep. If you would like the plant to grow larger the following year, transplant it to a larger pot in the fall.

HOW TO HARVEST

Most plants do best when you harvest whole stems. In the case of scented geraniums, however, a little goes a long way, so I sometimes choose big juicy leaves and pluck them from the main stem of the plant. If using several leaves, cut an entire stem from the plant, just above a leaf line.

Seeds, Seed Starting, and Propagation

SEEDS

Searching for and choosing which seeds to grow is definitely one of the best parts of gardening. There is something powerful about a seed packet full of possibility. It seems unlikely that a single small seed can produce enough food to put on your table, but it will. To have a hand in the process is nothing short of fascinating. The first time I planted a vegetable garden, I was surprised and awestruck that the plants actually sprouted and continued to grow. It was thrilling to see lettuces, leeks, and other small green shoots poke out of the rich, dark soil for the first time.

There are so many seed sources, from the nursery to the hardware store to mail order and online companies, that it can be challenging to choose the right seeds. As a general rule, try to purchase only organic seed. Several companies sell only organic seed that can be ordered online (check out the Resources, page 186).

By purchasing organic seed, you are supporting growers who have carefully bred seed for the best production. It is best to choose varieties adapted to your local conditions whenever possible. Plants evolve and change to accommodate their environment, so when you purchase seed that has been grown close to home (or grown in conditions similar to where you live), you're increasing your chances of success. Additionally, as big corporations continue to gain control over the vast majority of our seed options, purchasing organic helps keep diversity alive. Over the last several hundred years, we have lost a fair amount of genetic diversity in our seeds; as gardeners, we have the ability to play a key role in preserving that diversity. Organic seed, particularly from open-pollinated and heirloom varieties (more on this shortly), can also be harvested, saved, and replanted. Seed saving is an awesome process to observe and a great way to adapt seeds to your own microclimate. By saving seed year after year, seeds get conditioned to the specific garden space you grow in. Saving your own seed not only is an engrossing project, but also will help you to better understand the life cycle of a plant. And it's economical too!

When choosing seeds, be mindful of sow dates and maturing times. Many seed packets say "Sow after last frost," which is a vague time frame that can be confusing. In my view, seeds fall into three basic categories of planting times: those that can be planted first thing in spring, those that do well in heat (considered "heat tolerant"), and those that are good for cool-weather crops. For more specific information, it's best to consult a local planting calendar first rather than trying to deduce what to plant when based solely on the packet information. The days to maturity (that is, to harvest or flower blooming)—"50 days," "85 days"—give you a good frame of reference for the life cycle of your plant. This helpful information allows you to plan your garden around your schedule and make plans based on when you will be harvesting. For example, if you're planting lettuce in May and traveling for the month of July, you should steer clear of varieties with a 60-day maturity date.

Seed packets will also note whether the plant is open-pollinated, heirloom, or hybrid. Open-pollinated and heirloom seeds produce mature plants that create seeds that, when replanted, stay true to the parent plant. Opt for these varieties if you would like to save your seed. Hybrid plants have been cross-bred in some way, and if you save the seed, they will not consistently produce plants with the same qualities as the parent plant.

Because you are growing in small containers that essentially limit a plant's size, it is best to choose a smaller variety of plant whenever one is available. If dwarf varieties of your favorite vegetable are available, select those. It is also important to keep the climate in mind when purchasing seeds. For example, the Pacific Northwest has a short, cool summer season but mild winters, which allow year-round gardening of hardy greens and brassicas. Large melons, peppers, and corn are challenging to grow here. In contrast, Midwestern states have a long, hot summer season, ideal for tomatoes and peppers, but winters are generally too cold for unprotected outdoor crops. Be sure to follow the list of edible plants from the What to Grow for a Plentiful Harvest chapter (page 33). Start with those nearly foolproof basics and branch out in later years as you become more familiar with the practice of growing.

Seed Starting

I used to think starting plants from seed was a project best left to nurseries. My vision of small plants coming to life included rows and rows of seed trays set within the confines of the warm, steamy glass walls of a greenhouse. The process of seed starting always seemed elusive to me—even a little bit confusing. In truth, it is very easy to start your own seeds at home.

In the Pacific Northwest, where I tend gardens, in early spring it stays moist and cool, and our days are short. These conditions hinder germination of seeds. We have to wait for the ground to dry up and the sun to start shining to really take full advantage of the garden. The same goes for New England, though they have to wait for the ground to thaw. In stark contrast, gardeners in California can garden year-round. In every condition, however, starting seeds at home accelerates the process of growing.

There are clear benefits to seed starting. Starting seeds indoors will extend your growing season. When you start seeds in advance of their sow dates, you get a jump on the season. Instead of planting out seed directly in your garden, you plant an actual plant! This extra time means you'll be harvesting earlier. More importantly for home gardeners, though, starting your own seeds opens up a world of crops to you. Relying on nurseries and farmers to supply your plant starts means you get to choose only from what they decide to grow. Choosing your own varieties of vegetable from the pages of colorful catalogs is much more satisfying. You can experiment with varieties that are not well known and try something new. I always think, *why bother growing varieties that everyone else will grow?* I seek out something new every year. Additionally, it is more economical to buy seeds. One pack of lettuce seeds will have you in salad for the length of a season and costs about the same as one 4-inch pot of starts.

Many beginners trust that a sunny windowsill will receive enough light to grow plants. This is not always true. Southwest-facing windows will have the most exposure to sun, assuming your view is unobstructed and light flows freely in. Even then, depending on your latitude, in the dead of winter the sun is not out long enough to supply adequate light. Most apartments, therefore, don't have the perfect growing conditions and will need some supplies to mimic them.

Seedlings need light, warmth, moisture, and root nourishment to grow. You can start seeds in ordinary indoor light, but once they push up out of the soil, the seedlings need up to twelve hours of light daily to grow vigorously. In the northern hemisphere, we don't see that sort of natural light until well after the first day of spring, around March 21. But with the aid of grow lights, you can provide enough supplemental indoor light to convince seeds and seedlings that they're out in the sun. The fluorescent bulbs produce a light spectrum similar to that of the sun's rays. Grow lights can be picked up at most local hardware stores and plant shops. Grab the cheap version—a big bulb with a stainless steel shade or backing and a clip. (You can buy the hanging kind if you have the space and time to set up a system to hang it from.) The clip allows you to clamp the grow light onto a dining room chair or other sturdy support and focus the light directly on the seedlings. A timer for your light is also a good investment, unless you're an "early to bed, early to rise" type of person. You may have heard of people using a heat mat under their seed trays to warm the seed-starting medium, but I don't think this practice is really necessary for the casual gardener as long as your apartment is warm enough; plus, the grow light will offer some ambient heat.

Seed trays are a must for getting started. They provide the perfect depth for seedlings to grow strong before being transplanted, and you can sow an entire garden's worth of seeds in one go. Using one large seed tray also keeps the process a bit more organized and tidy. Plastic seed-starting trays are made from thin black plastic and have small cells to hold the seed-starting mix. I recommend using just one tray for your first year; it should provide enough space to produce plenty of plants for your garden. Be sure to also purchase the clear plastic cover that fits over each tray. This cover acts as insulation, keeping seeds warm and moist, which is the perfect condition for germination. You will also need the plastic liner tray for your seedling tray to sit in. This liner will catch and retain any excess water that drains, sparing spillage and helping to keep seedlings moist.

The seed cells should be filled with a sterile seed-starting mix—which technically is not a soil. These mixes often contain coco coir (coconut-shell fiber), pumice, and perlite. This combination allows for good drainage and air circulation and will readily absorb and retain water. There are no nutrients added to sterile seed mixes—seedlings do not need them at first as each seed has a small amount of food supply for the plant's early growth.

I set up seed trays on my dining room table in front of my only window—one that faces due east. Any table will do; just be certain you can plug in a grow light nearby. But ambient light from a window is always helpful, so place trays as close to natural light as possible. Rotate the seed tray every few days so plants will not stretch for the light and grow too leggy.

Once you have your seeds; tray, liner, and cover; grow light; seed-starting mix; and a dedicated space to grow in, it's time to start planting. The following is a step-by-step guide to starting your own seeds at home.

1 Cover the work surface with newspaper to catch any excess seed-starting mix. Fill the seed cells about three quarters of the way full with the mix. (You will be adding a bit more mix to cover the sown seeds.) It's easiest to sift seed-starting mix over the tops of the cells, then run your palm over the top of the cells to distribute evenly. This will also brush any excess mix from the divider rims into the cells.

2 Using a small water bottle, gently water the entire seed tray, making sure the mix gets thoroughly dampened. It's important to moisten the mix now so it can be weighed down and it has taken up some moisture. If you do this after you've sown your seeds, the water will pool on the surface of the mix, and seeds can easily spill up and over the sides of the plant cells. No big deal, but when a seed gets washed over into the next row, it does make for an interesting game of *what-the-hell-is-this-plant?* after germination.

3 Sow one or two seeds in each cell of the seedling tray, working in rows. I suggest planting only one variety of seed per row, even if you don't fill the row. This will help keep things organized.

4 Label your seeds as you go.

5 Lightly cover the entire surface with another sprinkle of seed-starting mix, and water very lightly again. As the bottom layer of mix is already moist, the top layer needs only a trickle. You can use a water bottle to spray a fine mist over the top of the seed tray; this gentle method won't disturb the surface or displace any seeds.

6 Cover the tray with the clear plastic top and slightly prop up one corner with a bottle cap or similar item for a bit of ventilation.

7   Set the tray directly under your grow light, and set your grow
     light to shine for twelve hours. Typically, I time the grow
     light to run from 6 a.m. to 6 p.m., making the most of natural
     daylight.

8   Keep the top layer of the mix just moist (not wet), never letting
     it dry out. The clear plastic cover will collect moisture from
     condensing evaporation. If there is no condensation on the
     inside of the plastic cover, that is usually a good indicator that
     you need to mist the tray with more water.

When seedlings are tall enough and hitting the sides of the cover, remove the cover and prepare to harden them off. *Hardening off* means gradually acclimating them to outside conditions. If you moved tender young plants from a warm environment immediately to a cool environment, they would go into shock and falter. Instead, you must help them slowly adjust to outside weather conditions. For the first three days of hardening off your seed tray, place it outside, sheltered from wind and rain, during the warmest part of the day for two hours. From the fourth to the sixth day, place your seed tray outside for four hours during the warmest part of the day. On the seventh and eighth days, place them outside for a total of six hours a day. You may have to adapt this depending on weather changes; use common sense. This practice should condition the starts enough to harden them off and prepare them for being planted out in containers.

If the current weather conditions are not conducive to planting out in the garden (too cold, too wet, and so on), instead of hardening off plants straight away, you can transplant (or *pot up*) the seedlings. Transplant the seedlings into small pots (4-inch pots from the nurseries work great) filled with regular potting soil, and keep them indoors under a grow light until the weather allows you to harden off the starts and plant them out.

Making Your Own Seed-Starting Mix

Seed-starting mix provides a sterile environment (seeds do not need nutrients during their early growth stage) and allows for air and moisture to pass easily through the growing medium. You can purchase commercial seed-starting mix, but the bags are often too big for the small amount needed. Years ago I started mixing my own from just three ingredients, and it works just as well. Coco coir is a nice, fluffy, fibrous ingredient that allows air and water to circulate around the seedlings. Perlite and pumice are both derived from volcanic rock and also help with drainage and air circulation. Making up small batches spares you from needing much storage space and is much less expensive.

WHAT YOU'LL NEED

- 3 parts coco coir
- 1 part perlite
- ½ part pumice

WHAT TO DO

In a deep bucket or large plastic bag, soak the brick of coco coir in 1 or 2 cups of water to moisten and reconstitute it. Add more water as needed, aiming to make the coco coir moist, but not wet. It will expand quite a bit, so use a container much larger than the brick. When the coco coir is ready, measure the parts and add the appropriate amounts of perlite and pumice. Stir thoroughly. Use the mix immediately for starting seeds. Any extra mix should be left to dry out somewhat, then stored until it is ready to use. At that time, add water to remoisten.

Seeds vs. Starts

Starting seeds at home is a lovely way to deeply connect you to your garden and the wonder of nature, but it's not the only way to get your apartment garden going.

Starts—immature potted plants—are an excellent way to grow food. They make it easy to plant and go, give you a jump start on the garden, and save you the time and effort of tending to seeds and seedlings. The one big down side that I can think of is that your options are restricted. If you want a particular variety or you want to grow something at a particular time when starts may not be available, you need to grow your own seedlings. Otherwise, choosing a plant start is fast, easy, and fun.

Purchase organic starts from a local nursery—they will offer plants fit for your climate right about the same time of year they are meant to be planted. Look for starts that appear healthy, with strong, vibrant leaves and thick stems. Pass over anything that looks wispy or limp. I like to turn over plant starts and inspect the bottom of the pot to see if any thick root structures have developed—an indication of an older plant that is potentially root-bound. I try to avoid these, if possible; if you end up with root-bound starts, just be sure to trim off the tangled root system before planting. This shouldn't harm the plant, and it gives them a nice, fresh start.

Propagation

Propagating a plant from a cutting or root division is one of the coolest parts of gardening. By doing this, you are splitting an existing plant into two or more. When I first tried my hand at propagation, of course I had no idea what I was doing. I clipped a stem off a scented geranium and stuck it inside a small pot filled

Plants to Propagate from Cuttings

- Lavender
- Lemon balm
- Mint
- Scented geraniums
- Tarragon

Herbs to Propagate by Root Division

- Chives
- Lovage
- Marjoram
- Oregano
- Thyme

with potting soil, watered often, and kept my fingers crossed—and it worked! I always feel like I'm getting away with something when I take a small piece from one plant to create a new plant. It's the ultimate garden share.

Propagating plants takes advantage of a plant's natural tendency to reproduce beyond the usual blooming and seeding. *Vegetative propagation* is an act of asexual reproduction (no seeds required), wherein a leaf, a small piece of root, or a stem will send down roots. This could be splitting the roots of a parent plant (root division) or taking a cutting. (Grafting is also considered a form of propagation, but you probably won't be starting an apple orchard on your patio anytime soon.) To foster this propagation, you must determine if your plant is a good candidate.

Many herbs can be divided by splitting their roots. To do this, dig up the plant and its entire root system as best you can in early spring or fall. Growth is slower during these seasons, which makes this treatment easier on the plant. Work apart the roots and slice through them with a clean knife or your hands. Be sure that each division has both healthy roots and at least one small green shoot.

Repot into a large enough pot and water well. Be sure to keep it watered well until the plant catches on and begins to put out new growth.

If you already have perennial herb pots going, it may be time for you to split them and separate the cuttings into two pots. Every three years or so perennial herbs do well with some dividing. Add some compost to the new potting mix and repot in the same-size container or larger. If you don't need more of the same herb, divide them anyway and repot some cuttings as gifts for friends or neighbors.

Some plants will root out from their stem, which makes them excellent candidates for cuttings. As a general rule of thumb, take a cutting from new plant growth. This is best done in mid- to late spring or early summer. Cuttings prosper in warm conditions. This also allows enough time for the cutting to put out some new growth without the stress and cold of winter. On some plants new growth comes in the form of a side shoot; in others it grows from the top of the plant's branches. Choose the newest growth and cut about a 5-inch length just below a set of leaves. Remove the lowest leaves from the cutting, as well as any buds or blossoms on the stem. (If left, these will take energy away from the plant by producing seed.) Place the cutting directly into a small pot of potting soil (leave it unfertilized for now), being sure to bury the lowest leaf node (the node is the area below the lowest leaves that you just removed) and water well. (The leaf node is where the bulk of the plant's hormones are located, and they will aid in root development.) Keep the cutting watered until the plant begins to put on new growth. When the cutting does not pull out of the soil with a gentle tug, new growth is sufficient for transplanting to a bigger pot; this generally takes from four to six weeks.

Cuttings are generally used to make new plants, but you can also use cuttings in a windowsill project like growing your food scraps; read more in Windowsill and Countertop Projects (page 173).

Self-Seeding Annuals

Self-seeding plants are a lazy gardener's dream come true. If you leave plants to flower and drop seed, odds are you'll end up with a brand-new crop of sprouts next spring.

Many edible flowers are self-seeding, which means you need only to let them reseed to gain many additional plants. When new sprouts grow, you can leave them to flourish, weed them out, or treat them as a hostess gift and repot for others.

Give self-seeding plants a nice big pot, or set an empty container with potting soil directly next to them so the seed has somewhere to drop and germinate come mid- to late summer. Here are some wonderful self-seeding edibles:

- Borage
- Chamomile
- Chervil
- Marigold
- Nasturtiums
- Nigella

Feeding and Watering Plants

When I first started gardening at home, I kept flowers that I thought were pretty or exceptionally fragrant. Without much consideration for their care, I put them in random pots I purchased, giving little thought to individual plant needs or my overall success at keeping them alive. As one might expect, I had plenty of failures and killed plants every year. At some point I decided that I should probably fertilize, so I did what many clueless but well-intentioned home gardeners do—I went to the store and bought a box of Miracle-Gro especially designed for flowers. Interestingly enough, the fertilizer looked like blue crystal. I wasn't sure what was in it, but I knew enough to be very careful not to let any come in contact with my skin. It was like a disco in a box—all bright neon and shiny. When I got home, I tried to follow the directions and add appropriate amounts of fertilizer to water, but really I just guessed and added a few mounded spoonfuls to my watering can. Looking back, it makes me cringe to think about all the chemicals I washed off my deck right into the waters of Lake Union, where I live. I didn't notice any marked difference in my garden that I recall, but it was the first time I considered how best to care for a plant.

Obvious statement number one: Plants are living things. Obvious statement number two: Because plants are living things, they need nourishment to grow and be healthy and productive. Just as we require a bare minimum of calories and hydration in order to survive, plants require certain essentials to put on healthy growth. These include minerals and other nutrients found in healthy soils, sunlight, and water. Without these key components, your plants will suffer.

Containers are not a natural environment in which to grow plants. Your goal as an urban gardener is to mimic their natural soil conditions within the confines of your pots. This entails a fine balance of fertilizer, water, and sun. Each plant has its own particular requirements, as well, so it can be a bit of a brain tease. As with most things, a little education up front will help you grasp how best to care for your plants.

Plants need three main nutrients in order to prosper: nitrogen, phosphorus, and potassium, represented on fertilizer labels by the elemental symbols from the periodic table: NPK. Different plants require varying levels of each. Certain plants are considered "heavy feeders." This refers to their dependence on a particular nutrient. Onions, for instance, are heavy feeders and will do best if given a regular supply of nutrients; in their case, chiefly nitrogen.

Because containers are continually being flushed (from watering), it's important to keep them on a regular feeding schedule. It is possible, however, to add too much fertilizer to your pots, leading to poor plant health and *burn*, which refers to the shriveled leaves indicative of overfertilization. With any garden, it is best to start out with small amounts of fertilizer and build up if your plants seem listless. In my own apartment garden, I generally add a teaspoon of fertilizer to small pots and a heaping tablespoon to large pots when I first plant or sow something. After that, plan to fertilize again about every eight weeks with a gentle organic fertilizer.

The following is a list of necessary nutrients, the role they play in plants, and some suggestions on adding them to your containers. This is not comprehensive, but all suggestions are organic, and easy enough to come by at your local nursery or by using your own resourcefulness.

NITROGEN (N)

In general, leafy green growth is supported by nitrogen. All plants need this, as they all have leafy greens that photosynthesize and convert sunlight to energy the plant then uses as food. Lettuces need a bit more nitrogen than, say, a tomato. We don't eat the green leaves of tomatoes, we eat the fruit; therefore super healthy green leaf support is not our top priority with a tomato plant. Lettuce, on the other hand, is a leafy green that we eat, so it's important to supply a healthy amount of nitrogen. Nitrogen should be added to pots every six to eight weeks. Constant watering will wash away the fertilizer over time. Take a small handful of fertilizer and dust it over the top surface of the soil, then gently work it in with a fork.

You can add nitrogen to your apartment garden in a number of ways.

Alfalfa Meal

Alfalfa meal is just that: ground-up alfalfa. These pellets release slowly into the soil over time and have a pretty low level of nitrogen, which is great for containers, as it helps to minimize burn. I use alfalfa meal in my pots often because it is considered a gentle fertilizer. This is also a good alternative to fish meal if you're a vegetarian.

Coffee Grounds

Coffee grounds are nitrogen rich and a great way to add nutrients to your soil without spending extra money on store-bought fertilizer. One pot of brewed coffee will render enough grounds to sprinkle on top of a large potted plant. Grounds may also act as a slug barrier (if you find slugs are an issue in your pots), as slugs don't like to slither over the rough texture. I use the grounds on most of my herbs. Take extra care if using on lettuces, however, because the grounds tend to get in between leaves and can sometimes scent them slightly. Coffee grounds will mix into your soil and break down over time. Coffee grounds also act as mulch (more about mulch shortly), so be careful to keep them away from direct contact with plant stems, which could lead to disease or decay as the grounds break down.

Fish Meal

Fish meal is made from ground-up fish and smells just as you'd think. Fishy! It's a great natural fertilizer made from what would otherwise be waste, and it is said to release slowly in your garden. Fish meal is great for pots that don't retain nutrients as natural soil will, and it's widely available and inexpensive. Many small nurseries carry it in bulk, so you can purchase it in small amounts as needed.

Grass Clippings

Green leafy plants contain nitrogen, remember? So grass clippings are an excellent source of natural nitrogen. Grab your lawn-mowing neighbor (preferably one who uses natural lawn care and doesn't spray pesticides) and arrange to pick up a yard waste bagful in the spring. It should last you at least through midsummer. Grass clippings can be placed on the surface of the pot's soil and left to break down. This decaying process has the added benefit of introducing microorganisms to your pots, which is good for your plants. For real. As with coffee grounds, be mindful to keep clippings away from direct contact with plant stems, where they can lead to disease or decay as they break down.

PHOSPHORUS (P)

Phosphorus promotes the healthy fruiting and flowering of plants by converting carbohydrates in the plants to sugars. If you think about it, snap peas, zucchini, and so on are all fruiting plants whose vegetables have a sweet taste. It's this conversion, helped by direct sun exposure, that is instigated by the presence of phosphorus.

Bone Meal

Bone meal has been used for years as a garden fertilizer. A slaughterhouse by-product, although bone meal may sound unappetizing, it is actually a great way to use something that would otherwise be wasted. Bones have a high calcium content, as well as some nitrogen.

Fish Bone Meal

This mixture is the same as bone meal, but made from the bones of fish.

Rock Phosphate

Vegetarians may balk at using meat and fish industry by-products, so I offer rock phosphate as a vegetarian solution for the vegetable garden. Rock phosphate is generally available in larger quantities, so it's admittedly cumbersome to store for the small apartment garden. Additionally, it is best used in actual garden topsoil (not in pots) because soil will hold onto this nutrient and slowly release it for years. In pots, this is not a perfect solution, as you will flush the soil through repeated watering and will likely be adding new soil to your pots each year. Still, it is not a bad option, should the other materials not appeal to you.

POTASSIUM (K)

Potassium encourages strong plant growth and a sturdy plant in general. When plants lack potassium, photosynthesis slows down and may weaken their stems. In fact, a weak plant stem is often an early sign of a potassium deficiency. I use potassium in all of my pots—a heaping tablespoon for the large pots and a teaspoon for the medium-sized to smaller pots. If I notice weak plant stems, I'll add a spoonful or two, as it's difficult to overfertilize with potassium. Here are two easy-to-find resources.

Granite Dust

Just as the name implies, this dust is collected at quarries as a by-product. Granite will help build reserves of potassium in your plants, but it's a long, slow process, so it makes sense to use only in your largest pots. Considering that, I much prefer kelp meal.

Kelp Meal

Harvested from the sea, kelp meal is dried and ground up seaweed. It is complete with an abundance of trace minerals, which is also good for the garden. (Remember, plants take up nutrients through their roots, so in theory any nutrients you add to the soil will be taken up by the root and eventually ingested by *you*!) Not only will kelp meal add these micronutrients to your food, but it also supplies a small amount of potassium to your plants. Even better, kelp meal is widely available and can often be found in bulk.

MICROORGANISMS—
The Good Bacteria

It is also important to try to introduce microorganisms to your pots when you can. Microorganisms—composed of bacteria and fungi, among others—have several different functions in the garden. They aerate soil, break down organic matter so it is easily digestible to plants, and support healthy root systems. Containers do not naturally invite decomposers and microorganisms to them, as the purchased potting medium is not part of a functioning ecosystem. When is the last time you saw an earthworm in a pot? Although it's a challenge to get these tiny helpers into your container garden, you can increase your odds by creating an environment that will attract them.

Microorganisms are attracted to the decomposition of organic matter. In fact, they aid in that process, and the results will ultimately feed your plants. To manufacture a hospitable environment, you need only introduce a steady supply of organic matter and, even better, decaying or decayed organic matter. You can do this by adding "greens" or other organic matter to your pots. Greens come in the form of chopped weeds and, as mentioned earlier, lawn clippings and spent coffee grounds. Sprinkle a handful over the top of the soil around the base of your plants (carefully leaving the area right around the plant stems bare). Over time, without any maintenance, these added greens will start to break down and decompose. Eventually you can fork this decomposed matter into your potting soil and continue adding more on top. Microorganism activity increases with the ambient temperature. The work they do grinds to a halt in winter, as both plants and organisms fall dormant, and begins to pick up again in spring. Activity will continue to increase as temperatures rise into the summer, so be sure to gather greens to keep on hand for adding to your pots during the warmer months. I typically fill a large yard-waste bag full of grass clippings in spring (from a friend's yard) and keep it handy on my deck.

Green Manure

"Green manure" is a term used for a fast-growing cover crop (a crop used to cover bare earth) that is eventually turned under into the soil to decay, like compost. In this fashion, microorganisms and nutrients are added to the soil. For a container gardener, this concept is a bit much to put into practice; it's easier to sprinkle a handful of compost or coffee grounds in your containers.

But green manure does more than add nutrients. Growing a complementary green at the base of other crops suppresses weeds (and yes, weeds *will* find their way into your containers!), helps to hold in water, and contributes to aerating the soil. These crops also help regulate soil temperature, keeping it warmer in winter and cooler in summer. Green manure is also beneficial if you choose a flowering cover crop like buckwheat. For larger plants, like cucumbers, I often distribute a few pinches of buckwheat seed along the perimeter of the container. For a container with a smaller plant, like lettuce, try Huia white clover, which grows densely but not tall enough to block sun from the lettuce plants.

Winter Mulching

In winter, I switch over to a brown mulch—a more durable organic material that will hold up and insulate my plants in the cooler months. Winter mulches prevent nutrients from being leached out of the pot and help minimize compaction from winter snow and rain. In an in-ground garden plot, winter mulches are very important. For a container garden, winter mulches act more as insulation to protect perennial plant roots from freezing temperatures.

Fallen leaves are readily available and easy to come by, and you can spread them across the entire container surface to protect the potting soil. They will likely not decompose over winter, so come spring be sure to remove them from the containers and put them in your regular compost. Cardboard and newspaper also work well; you can shred or tear them and lay them directly on the soil surface. Use only the black-and-white newsprint, as colored ink can be harmful. Shredded paper will break down rather quickly, so you can leave any residual paper come spring and it will soon decay, at which point you can dig it into the soil like compost.

HOME COMPOSTING

Compost, as any gardener will tell you, is one of the single most important additions to a healthy, sustainable garden. It is the great equalizer, taking in the bad and processing it into something good.

What follows may be a bit overwhelming for the casual gardener, but as you dig in you will learn that compost is truly fascinating. This lush brown medium acts as fertilizer, insulates plants, suppresses weeds, and retains moisture. Although a small-scale urban gardener growing plants in pots doesn't necessarily have to devote a lot of thought to compost, it's nice to understand just what it is and how it can work for you so you can make educated choices about when to use it and why.

Compost is essentially made up of organic matter (from plants and animals) that has been broken down over time. There are many players in this process—animals, fungi, bugs, microbes, bacteria—all of whom play a part in the decomposition of organic matter that results in compost.

There are two basic methods for making compost: hot and cold. A hot compost pile produces *finished* compost (ready for garden use) more quickly. The hot composting method generates internal heat, which accelerates the process of breaking down the organic matter. Using the right mixture of carbon and nitrogen (that is, browns like dried leaves and greens like lawn clippings), hot compost heats up by feeding on carbon. When it eventually burns out, nitrogen-rich compounds are left behind. Now, if you've been reading straight through from the beginning, you know that leafy greens need nitrogen to grow strong, productive plants. So this hot-processed compost is a very beneficial addition to any garden.

Cold compost is created in the same way as hot compost, but at a much slower rate, as it is a passive process. Cold compost does not "burn" carbon, but instead relies on the slow work of decomposers to break down organic matter and convert it into compost over time.

Of the two processes, cold compost is certainly the easiest. You simply dig a hole in the ground and add vegetable food waste and green and brown yard waste, then cover it up.

In a small garden, however—particularly one with no actual garden soil—none of these processes are really possible. But that doesn't necessarily exclude an urban gardener from the compost game. *Vermiculture* is another great resource for making compost at home in a very small space. Vermiculture uses worms in a worm bin to break down food waste and bedding into compost. Worms produce castings: worm manure, also called *vermicompost*. These castings are then collected and used on plants and in gardens as lush, nitrogen-dense fertilizer.

A worm bin has the added benefit of being small; it can be stored inside or outside. So it's an excellent option for apartment and condo dwellers who want to compost at home.

Worms can eat half their weight in food waste every day. If you start off with 1 pound of worms, count on their handling about ½ pound of kitchen scraps each day. There are a number of options for worm bins, from pricey commercial bins with multiple trays to plastic storage bins or homemade bins. All systems need some method of drainage, because worms generate liquid waste, and if conditions get too mucky, the worms will not be happy. The worms used in worm bins are not your garden earthworms, but a particular species—commonly called red worms or red wigglers—that would not survive for long in outdoor conditions. You can buy them locally or by mail order, but the cheapest (free!) source is from a gardener who already has a worm bin going.

It is important to note that a new worm bin starts off slowly, so you should add food waste in small amounts at first and monitor how quickly the worms are able to process them. They may ignore foods they don't like; if so, remove these scraps from the bin so they don't rot and give off odors. When you add food to the bin, lift some of the shredded newspaper bedding, put food scraps underneath, then cover with the bedding. This will help minimize odors. Add the scraps in a different part of the bin each time, so the worms have a chance to process the older scraps before more waste is piled over them. Plan to follow a pattern, moving from left to right and then right to left, back and forth through the bin.

Worms can get finicky about what they will or won't eat. A few finely crushed eggshells provide grit to help them digest, as worms do not have teeth. Do not give the worms proteins, dairy, oil, or oily products like vegetables cooked in oil or fried potato chips. Give them plant-based organic matter like vegetable and fruit scraps. Worms especially love soft, mushy materials. The usual advice is to skip citrus peel, because it's hard for worms to consume, but they just need to soften and decompose. Worms also love coffee grounds, and you can include the paper filters. Grains (stale bread, tortillas, and so on) are OK too.

Keep your worms in a temperate location, ranging from 55 degrees F to 75 degrees F; this means you may need to bring an outdoor bin inside during cold winter months.

After a few months, the worm compost will likely appear dark brown, like finely crushed cookie crumbs. This can take up to six months. To harvest compost and replenish the bedding, move the entire contents of the bin over to one side. On the other side, refill the area with a mound of fresh bedding. Add some new kitchen waste to the new bedding side (close to the old bedding with the worms) and wait for the worms to migrate over. This can take

anywhere from two weeks to the better part of a month. Worm compost can be used on all potted plants and even indoor plants. Top-dress your pots with a sprinkling of worm compost every six weeks or so. As worm castings are quite nutrient rich, you want to be sure not to add too much too often or you run the risk of plant burn from overfertilization.

As mentioned earlier, worms also expel liquid as they work to break down your kitchen scraps. You can collect that liquid and add it directly to plants along with the vermicompost. Or add an equal part of water to the worm "tea" and spray or water your plants with this solution. This also makes a great gift for any gardeners in your life.

WATERING SCHEDULE

Water, it is quite obvious, is crucial to healthy plant growth and a successful garden. Water transports minerals to the plant, allows evaporation for cooling, and aids in photosynthesis. Plants confined in containers will need extra attention, as water drains out quickly and pots expose individual plants to more sun, wind, and heat than in a traditional garden environment. Water may also evaporate from pots, which is why container material (see page 11) also plays a role in determining the water needs for each plant. Given that, there are some basic principles to follow when watering your containers.

Rule #1: Water Regularly

It is imperative that you never let potting soil go completely dry at any point in a plant's life cycle. Allowing your potting soil to get bone dry increases the odds of soil compaction, further reducing the odds of water retention. With a compacted potted plant, water will often collect on the surface and pool down the sides of a container instead of moistening the soil uniformly. Any medium with peat is particularly susceptible to compaction. To avoid drying out your pots, be sure to check for water daily by inserting a finger into the pot. Soil should feel damp (not overly wet) about 2 inches down. If the soil is dry, water.

Rule #2: Water Deeply

Add enough water to your pots that some water seeps out of the drainage holes. This indicates a full watering, and the roots in the bottom of the container can take up water. If you water only to a shallow depth, you encourage the plant to have shallow roots. Shallow roots lead to a weakened plant. And a weakened plant will have a diminished harvest. It's a bad cycle to start, and it is challenging to eradicate. It is better to water fully and deeply every two to three days than to give your plants a little sprinkle every day.

Rule #3: Do Not Overwater

Overwatering plants waterlogs the soil and prohibits oxygen from flowing freely to their roots. Plants need oxygen to survive, so this is a serious problem. In a short time, waterlogging leads to decay and rot. Not good. To ensure that you do not overwater your plants, check for dryness in the soil before you water. Also, make sure you have proper drainage and that water is flowing through your container. You can also check the bottom of your pots for excess moisture. Turn the pots over every now and then and feel through the drainage holes for dampness. If the soil is too wet, give it a day or two to be absorbed by the plant and evaporated before watering again.

Rule #4: Timing Is Everything

Plants' water needs change with the seasons and depend on sun exposure, temperature, and the size and material of your container, so there is no hard and fast rule on how often you should water. Keeping these variables in mind, you can develop the best watering schedule for your plants. The seasons often dictate a commonsense approach. Plants need more water in summer (when it is hot, and soil dries out faster) than in fall (when the days are shorter and cooler). In fact, some container plants may need two daily waterings in summer, depending on your sun exposure. Rooftop containers will get much warmer than those on an east-facing balcony. Use your best judgment. As a general rule, plants will do much better if you water first thing in the morning before it gets too warm. This allows for a proper soaking and avoids immediate evaporation due to heat. It also allows time for water to work its way through the pot so that you are not causing "wet feet" or overly damp roots in the cool of night. In some regions, cold nights will cool wet soil and stress heat-lovers like beans, zucchini, and cucumbers. Conversely, leafy greens often appreciate an early-evening cool-down (and will show signs of water and heat stress by wilting and shriveling along the leaves' edges). Plan to check your plants every morning, water if they need it, and water in the evening only if a plant is really suffering from heat, which can happen in the height of summer.

Rule #5: Find a Friend to Help

If you leave town in summer, you must find someone to water your plants. You can set up your own self-watering system at home for short weekend jaunts (see Water Bottle Redux project below), but if you're taking a holiday in the high season of summer, make sure to have a friend or neighbor come over and water. It is quite possible for plants to die in a matter of days if not properly watered when it's consistently hot out, so do yourself a favor and have someone tend the garden for you. You can always trade them some homegrown goodies for their efforts.

WATER BOTTLE REDUX

Never one to toss something out without first considering how I can use it, I have made plastic water bottles the tool du jour in my garden. I use them to water my plants, protect seedlings, and, in a pinch, act as a drip system when I'm away for some time.

A *cloche* is a protective dome of plastic or glass that insulates plants and protects them from inclement weather so that they can grow with vigor. The original cloches were bell jars, beautiful glass domes with ventilation at the top. Cloches are set directly over individual plants, where they trap in heat from the sun and protect from wind, rain, and even some pests. You can emulate the concept of a bell jar by using a water jug or bottle.

A drip system or sprinkler is a timed watering mechanism for gardens. Obviously, most apartment gardens will not have a drip system, and there is not always a willing neighbor to water when you're away. In the heat of summer, it is crucial that your plants receive regular water. You do not want the soil to dry out—it will grow hard and will not allow water to pass through evenly. To prevent this, set up a slow drip water system when you're gone and no one is around to pitch in. It's not a perfect solution, but it's a good one.

Here are the how-tos for reusing and recycling water bottles in the garden.

Water Bottle Cloche

Trim off the bottom of your water jug or bottle as close to the bottom as possible. Set the water bottle directly over seedlings or starts and push the cut rim into the soil to anchor. Leave the cap off to allow for ventilation.

Water Bottle Watering

Use a water bottle with a cap. Trim the bottom off the bottle. Take the water bottle cap and pierce a hole in the top with a small nail and a hammer. You can also use a thin drill bit (about ⅛ inch). Test for drainage by putting water in the open end of the water bottle and holding it upside down. The water should come out at a slow trickle—a drop every few seconds. Submerge the water bottle, cap side down, into your pot. Fill the bottom with water to the rim. Refill as needed.

Seasonal Care

It's pretty straightforward to tend plants during spring and summer—fill container, plant, feed, water. But how do you care for plants in the off season?

1   At the end of the growing cycle (end of summer or early autumn), empty the pots of all annual plants, composting dead leaves, stems, and roots.

2   Clear out all root structures from the soil in pots. I lay out a tarp or large sheet on my balcony and turn the pots over, hand-comb out the roots, and then pour the soil back into the pot.

3   For winter, stack pots and store them out of sight, leaving behind any residual soil. When next you plant, freshen up this soil with half organic compost and half potting soil. You will do this every year, changing out and rotating your growing medium.

4   For perennial plants, be sure to mulch the soil by November. You can use a compost, a layer of dead leaves, bark mulch, or even hay or dead twigs. If you're able to move pots into a covered area of your garage (if you have one), that's brilliant. If I don't have a storage area, and I know we're heading for a cold winter, I will wrap my pots in burlap to warm them up ever so slightly and protect them from freezing temperatures. I talk to the plants every autumn and let them know I'd like them to live over the winter and come back in the spring, but other than mulch and a blanket, they'll have to fend for themselves.

5   Be sure to water perennial plants over winter, particularly if they are under cover and not receiving any water from rain or snow. I do this once a month, adding a glassful of water to each pot.

FEEDING AND WATERING PLANTS

Recipes from the Garden

Keeping a patio garden is a labor of love. Containers need more attention than a garden plot does. Sun exposure is often limited, watering must be monitored almost daily, and efficient use of limited space can be a challenge. Speaking for myself, there is a lot of tripping over pots and materials on my deck! In the end, however, it is worth it. I experience sweet satisfaction every time I harvest something from my garden and make a meal. It is refreshing to not have to run to the store for something green. It's also very nice to be influenced by what's available. I don't always know what to make for a meal, but with a quick glance out to the garden, I often find an answer or, at the very least, inspiration.

Plants do better when you actively harvest from them or prune them back. Most plants continue putting on growth and bearing fruit when harvested regularly. This is a good thing, as it means the kitchen is in constant supply in the high season of summer.

Once you have your own garden going, you'll learn that plants will dictate what you're eating, not the other way around. Lettuce is ready when it's ready, so now you get to enjoy a salad. Borage leaves are young and tender for only a few weeks, so during that time you had best figure out how to incorporate them into your meals. If you let these windows of opportunity pass you by, you run the risk of bolted, bitter, or poorly flavored food.

When thinking about garden recipes, I follow a few basic principles. I like to keep it fresh and let flavors shine through. For me, the simpler the recipe, the better. My guess is that most people don't like overly complicated food, and when you're cooking with herbs and flowers you needn't do much to highlight their flavor. I also like to use as much of the plant as possible. Stems, leaves, flowers, all of it. If I let something go too long and its leaves are yellowed, I use that, too. Make it your goal to leverage all the energy you've put into keeping the plant alive and well; you can do this by using every last bit to your advantage.

Admittedly, some of the plants in the What to Grow for a Plentiful Harvest chapter are not familiar choices for most people. I've included a lot of flowers and herbs because those plants do well in containers. They may well be completely new to you, and so we get to the adventure of experimentation in the garden and the kitchen. This is a great opportunity to expand your horizons and try something new. Eat something different. Challenge your palate in a new way. Make sure to pick leaves off your edible plants as they grow to see what they taste like. Only you know what you like!

I have included recipes that are both simple and delicious. The recipes are seasonal as well, drawing on crops that will be ready at the same time. For example, zucchini comes in right about the time that borage is vigorous, so I came up with a simple tart recipe using both that you can make for an appetizer, lunch, or light dinner. In a perfect world, all ingredients should work together as a seasonal dish. Each recipe is followed by some suggestions for incorporating your harvest into other meals. Try them all.

Zucchini Fritters

This is an easy recipe to use up a garden glut of zucchini (a wonderful container plant) and odds and ends of herbs you have growing. It's also light and summery. Feel free to experiment with the herbs you use, but go for a mix of tender herbs (such as mint or tarragon) rather than those that do better with some cooking time (like the hardier sage and thyme). The recipe multiplies easily, so you can also adjust the quantity of this dish up, given the number of guests you're feeding.

MAKES 4 TO 6 FRITTERS

- 3 tablespoons olive oil, plus more for frying
- ½ onion, finely chopped (about 1 cup)
- Kosher salt
- 2 cups finely diced zucchini (about 2 medium)
- 2 eggs
- 2 tablespoons flour, all-purpose or whole wheat
- ¼ teaspoon freshly ground black pepper
- ¼ cup chopped fresh herb mix—mint, anise hyssop, tarragon

1   Place a large sauté pan over medium heat and add the 3 tablespoons of olive oil. Add the onions and a pinch of salt. Sauté until the onions are soft and translucent, 8 to 10 minutes. Add the zucchini and another pinch of salt. Sauté until the zucchini is soft and nearly cooked through, another 3 minutes. Remove from the heat and spread in a single layer on a sheet pan to cool to room temperature. →

2   In a medium bowl, whisk together the eggs, flour, pepper, and herbs. Fold the cooled zucchini mixture into the eggs until all has been incorporated. You should have a thin batter that holds together but is loose.

3   Heat a large skillet over medium heat and cover the bottom with a thin layer of olive oil. When the pan is hot, add small ladles full of zucchini batter to form fritters about 4 inches in diameter. Fry on both sides, about 4 to 5 minutes per side, until golden brown. Repeat with the remaining batter. Serve immediately.

MORE GARDEN RECIPES: Zucchini tastes great raw and is wonderful in summertime salads. For a quick panzanella salad (bread salad), cut zucchini into small cubes and toss with some crushed tomatoes, croutons, mint, and basil, and dress simply with olive oil and red wine vinegar.

Chive Butter and Radish Toasts

This appetizer is a simple way to pull together a little nosh for guests if you're in a pinch for time. Chives and radishes are among the first vegetables available in spring. Garnish with some edible flowers if desired.

MAKES 24 TOASTS

- 2 tablespoons finely chopped chives
- 4 tablespoons unsalted butter, at room temperature
- Baguette, cut into thin slices
- 1 bunch radishes, trimmed of greens and washed well
- Coarse sea salt

1 Preheat the oven to 400 degrees F. Combine the chives and butter in a small bowl and mash together with the back of a spoon until well blended. Refrigerate to firm up.

2 Lay the baguette slices in a single layer on a large sheet pan and bake until crispy and just beginning to brown at the edges, about 12 minutes. Remove and let cool completely. While the toasts are cooling, slice the radishes using the thinnest setting of a mandoline. If you don't have a mandoline, slice them with a knife as thinly as possible, so they're almost see-through. When the toasts are completely cooled, smear the tops with a thin layer of chive butter. Lay the radish slices on top, overlapping the layers slightly. Sprinkle with sea salt and set on a platter.

3 Continue layering toasts, chive butter, radishes, and salt until you run out of radishes. Serve immediately. Store any leftover chive butter, wrapped tightly in plastic wrap, in your freezer.

Salt and Nigella Flatbread

This quick recipe can be whipped together in a hurry. These flatbreads are reminiscent of pita bread, but not nearly as doughy. They are made with whole wheat flour, which makes them dense and hearty. Nigella seeds have a slight onion taste and make a beautiful garnish for this flatbread.

MAKES 10 TO 12 FLATBREADS

- 1½ cups whole wheat flour
- ½ cup all-purpose flour
- 1 tablespoon olive oil, plus more for brushing (or melted butter)
- Scant ¾ cup warm water
- Coarse sea salt
- 2 tablespoons nigella seeds

1   Combine the flours, olive oil, and water in the bowl of an electric mixer fitted with a dough hook and knead on the medium-slow setting for 5 to 7 minutes, until all the flour is incorporated and the dough is elastic, not wet. Remove from the bowl, cover with a cloth, and set aside to rest for one hour.

2   Preheat the oven to 400 degrees F. Set a sheet pan in the oven to heat. Cut off pieces of dough to form small balls—about the size of a ping-pong ball. On a lightly floured surface, roll each ball into a thin flat disk, about 5 inches across. When you have five or six disks of dough, remove the sheet pan from the oven and place the disks on the hot pan. Return the pan to the oven and bake until the edges are just golden brown, 8 to 10 minutes. Continue baking the rest of the dough in this fashion. →

3   While the flatbreads are still warm, brush one side with olive oil, sprinkle with salt, and finish with a sprinkling of nigella seeds. Serve warm or hold at room temperature.

MORE GARDEN RECIPES: Nigella seeds make wonderful garnishes for soups or savory vegetable dishes. Crushed into a paste, they also pair nicely with cooked-down plums as a side dish for a cheese plate.

Pea Vine Dumplings

Many cultures include savory cakes and dumplings in their cuisine. My family in Croatia eats *burek*—a strudel-like dough stuffed with a savory filling like meat and onion, or something sweet like apples. When I was little, my Aunt Janet used to fry us up some *frites* filled with ham and mozzarella, just as she had learned from her Italian mother-in-law. Really, any dough stuffed with something and fried is guaranteed to be the bomb.

Pea plants are easy to grow in containers, and while you grow them for the peas, you can also clip tender vines from the plant to sauté. This recipe takes that one step further and makes use of older pea vines that are strong and slightly woody. Normally we would never eat them, but broken down and cooked in this recipe, they shine. These fried dumplings are a great way to use the entire plant. You can use other hardy greens for this recipe—wild dandelion greens would work. (If they are very bitter, temper their bite with a sweet vinegar like sherry or some honey before adding to the dumplings.)

This is a dumpling dough, not a yeasted dough, so it will not be soft and flaky. Be sure to let the dough rest for at least an hour before shaping and frying. If you don't want to be stuck waiting while the dough rests, make it the night before, cover it with plastic wrap, and leave it on the counter overnight. →

Dough

- ½ cup all-purpose flour
- ½ cup whole wheat pastry flour
- Pinch of kosher salt
- ¼ to ½ cup warm water

Filling

- 2 tablespoons olive oil
- ½ onion, finely chopped (about 1 cup)
- ½ pound pea vines, coarsely chopped (about 4 cups)
- Scant ½ cup water
- ¼ teaspoon ground cumin
- ¼ teaspoon ground coriander
- ¼ teaspoon smoked paprika
- Kosher salt and freshly ground black pepper
- Vegetable oil for frying

1   Mix the flours and salt in large bowl or pulse in the bowl of an electric mixer. Add the water in increments and work in by hand until the dough comes together, or, with the mixer running, add a little bit of water at a time until the dough comes together in one ball. Once the dough forms a ball, knead on a floured work surface until the dough is elastic and smooth, about 10 minutes. Cover with plastic wrap or a damp towel and let sit on the counter for at least an hour, up to overnight.

2   To make the filling, cover the bottom of a large sauté pan with the olive oil and set over medium-high heat. Add half of the onions and all of the pea vines and cook, stirring often, so the pea vines and onions do not stick. Once the pea vines are fairly broken down and the onions are beginning to soften, add the water and turn the heat up to high. Bring to a boil, then reduce the heat to a simmer and cover the pan. (Because the pea vines are thick and woody, you are cooking them down to soften them.)

3   Cook, covered, until the pea vines are soft and the water is nearly evaporated, 15 to 20 minutes. Remove the lid and turn up the heat to dry out the greens and onions and steam off any

extra water. Stir often. When the pan is dry and the greens are beginning to stick, transfer the mixture to a large bowl. Add the remaining onions, cumin, coriander, and paprika. Season to taste with salt and pepper and let cool.

4   To make the dumplings, cut the dough into twelve pieces and roll into balls between your palms. Lightly flour your hands if the dough sticks. On a lightly floured work surface, roll out balls of dough into small rounds 4 or 5 inches in diameter.

5   Working with one round at a time, place a spoonful of pea vine filling in the center. Fold the dough in half. Working from the middle out, press the sides together to create a seal. (By doing this, you are pushing out any air, to prevent the dumplings from breaking open while they're frying.) You can pinch the edges with your fingers or use the back of a fork to press a design in the dough and make sure the seal holds.

6   Over medium-high heat, heat about 1 inch of vegetable oil in a deep-sided sauté pan. When the oil is hot, but not smoking, slip in about four dumplings—as many as will fit without overcrowding—and fry until golden brown, 4 to 5 minutes. Flip over with a slotted spoon and fry the other side until golden brown, about another 5 minutes. Lift out with a slotted spoon and drain on a paper bag. Fry the remaining dumplings and serve hot or at room temperature.

7   The dumplings can be made several hours ahead and fried when ready, or frozen, wrapped tightly in a plastic bag, to fry at a later date.

MORE GARDEN RECIPES: Older pea vines can also be cooked as described here and used as a side dish. Omit the spices and instead add a handful of toasted pine nuts and a squeeze of lemon juice.

Crispy Marjoram Potatoes

This is one of my favorite ways to cook potatoes. The trick is to put the potatoes cut side down in a sauté pan over medium heat (not hotter or they'll burn!) and leave them be. No touching! The potatoes end up golden brown and crispy but remain fluffy and sweet inside like a mashed potato. Potatoes and marjoram are a great match. For this recipe, I cook half the marjoram with the potatoes and add half to the finished dish for extra herby flavor. You can double up this batch to serve a crowd, but make sure you keep the potatoes in a single layer in the pan. You may need to use two pans to accommodate them all.

SERVES 4

- 2 tablespoons olive oil
- 1 tablespoon butter
- 1 pound Yukon Gold or fingerling potatoes, sliced in half lengthwise
- 2 tablespoons chopped fresh marjoram, divided
- Kosher salt
- Freshly ground black pepper

1   Preheat the oven to 350 degrees F. In a large ovenproof sauté pan over medium heat, heat the olive oil and butter. When the butter is melted and hot, add the potatoes to the pan in a single layer, cut side down. Sprinkle with some salt and cook until a sharp knife almost pierces the center, 8 to 10 minutes. The potatoes will still give resistance and be raw in the middle. Sprinkle 1 tablespoon of the marjoram over the potatoes and place the entire pan in the oven.

2   Bake until a sharp knife easily pierces through the flesh, 10 to 15 minutes. Remove from the oven and transfer to a shallow serving bowl. Toss in the remaining marjoram and stir to combine. Season to taste with salt and pepper and serve.

MORE GARDEN RECIPES: Marjoram is a natural herb for any Italian dish. For a quick tomato sauce, sauté chopped garlic in olive oil, add a can or jar of stewed tomatoes, and finish it with a few tablespoons of marjoram. Marjoram also tastes great with chicken; try substituting marjoram in the Thyme-Roasted Chicken Legs with Charred Onions recipe (page 140).

Smoky Chickpeas with Greens

Arugula is one of the first greens to pop up in late winter or early spring, so it is perfect for a garden salad after months of no fresh greens. The greens are strong tasting and bitter—an excellent addition to legume salads. In this recipe, the acid from a lemon cuts the bite from the raw onion. The addition of chickpeas makes for a light lunch. This is an easy recipe to multiply for guests.

SERVES 1

- 3 thin slices red onion
- ½ lemon, zested and juiced
- 3 tablespoons olive oil
- ¼ teaspoon smoked paprika
- ¼ teaspoon kosher salt
- ½ cup chickpeas, cooked
- 1 cup arugula or other lettuces
- Freshly ground black pepper

In large bowl, combine the onion and lemon juice. Let stand for 5 to 10 minutes. Then add the lemon zest, olive oil, paprika, salt, and chickpeas. Stir well and let sit for at least 15 minutes. Toss in the arugula and stir to blend. Season to taste with salt and pepper and serve immediately.

MORE GARDEN RECIPES: Arugula goes nicely with other early and hearty greens like miner's lettuce. Make a simple salad using both greens and whatever herbs you have around. Arugula is also a decent substitute for watercress in recipes. Try adding some leaves to a creamy potato soup and blending.

Pickled Cucumber and Toasted Sesame Salad

I make this salad all the time, and my friends are always calling me for the recipe. Typically, they're shocked to find out how few ingredients there are. "That's it?" they all ask in disbelief. Essentially what you're doing is quickly pickling the cucumbers in rice wine vinegar. The added touch of toasty flavor comes from both sesame oil and toasted sesame seeds. You could easily forgo the seeds if you don't have them handy.

SERVES 2 TO 4

- 3 tablespoons rice wine vinegar
- 2 teaspoons sugar
- 1 pound cucumbers, peeled and cut into thin slices
- 1 teaspoon sesame oil
- 1 teaspoon sesame seeds, toasted

In a shallow bowl, combine the vinegar and sugar. Add the cucumbers and toss to coat. Set aside to macerate for 30 minutes or so, stirring often to rotate the cucumber slices. After 30 minutes, add the sesame oil and toasted sesame seeds. Stir to combine and serve.

MORE GARDEN RECIPES: Cucumbers can be finely diced and combined with tarragon for a relish on grilled fish in the summer. Or chop cucumbers finely and stir with some plain yogurt for a dipping sauce for zucchini fritters. In a fresh salad or raw soup, cucumbers also pair nicely with melons.

Minted Arugula Salad

Arugula and mint work beautifully together: one leaf is spicy, the other cooling. This salad can be chopped fine and used as a garnish on sliced tomatoes or grilled meat. The two can be blended into a pesto for marinating fish or tossing with pasta. (Both of those variations will require a bit more olive oil than indicated here.) Another option is to leave the greens whole, as I've done here for a side salad. Feel free to play with the proportions. Salads are meant to be easy affairs. I seldom measure ingredients; I just figure one handful of greens per person.

SERVES 2 AS A SMALL SALAD

- 1 cup arugula
- ¼ cup mint leaves, torn
- 2 tablespoons olive oil
- ½ lemon, zested and juiced
- Kosher salt and freshly ground black pepper

Place the arugula, mint, olive oil, lemon juice, and lemon zest in a large mixing bowl and toss to blend. Season to taste with salt and pepper. Serve immediately.

MORE GARDEN RECIPES: Arugula is a great green to add flavor and texture to your salads. If your plant goes to flower, pick off small leaves and use the white flower heads in salads. Because its flavor is so strong, you can also incorporate arugula into soups. Make a white bean soup and add a handful or two of arugula when you blend it smooth. It adds a nice spicy note.

Fresh Snap Pea and Potato Salad

Teeny-tiny spring potatoes can be ready as early as May and make a lovely addition to this salad. Here, cooked potatoes are tossed with chopped snap peas and spring chive blossoms, which are plump and blooming in May. This fresh-tasting, crisp salad is excellent served with a sweet grilled sausage for dinner, or a hard-boiled egg and some olives for a healthy lunch. You may alter the flavor by varying the herbs or the vinegar you use.

SERVES 4

- 1 pound spring potatoes, washed
- 2 tablespoons kosher salt
- 2 tablespoons minced shallot
- 1 tablespoon red wine vinegar
- ½ pound snap peas, ends trimmed

- 1 tablespoon Dijon mustard
- 3 tablespoons olive oil
- ¼ teaspoon freshly ground black pepper
- 3 tablespoons chive blossom petals
- Mixed herb leaves, for garnish (optional)

1   Set a large pot of water over high heat, add the potatoes and salt, and cover. Bring the potatoes to a boil. Reduce the heat slightly and cook until the potatoes are just tender, 20 to 25 minutes.

2   While the potatoes are cooking, put the shallot and vinegar in a large salad bowl and let sit for 5 minutes to macerate. After 5 minutes, add the snap peas, Dijon, oil, and pepper to the bowl, and stir well with a fork to emulsify the dressing and coat the peas.

3   Once the potatoes are tender, drain and add the still-warm potatoes to the salad bowl. Using a large spoon, fold gently to combine. Taste for seasoning and add the chive blossoms and any other herbs you choose to include. Serve immediately.

Tomato Chips

This is one of my most favorite recipes to make when tomatoes ripen. These thin slivers of dried, flavorful tomatoes are *so* delicious, excellent for snacking, and texturally satisfying, and they make a beautiful appetizer for winter dinner parties.

SERVES MANY (FIGURE 1 TOMATO PER SERVING)

- Any paste tomato, like Roma, cut into ½-inch-thick slices
- Olive oil
- Kosher salt
- 1 or 2 stems of thyme or lemon thyme, leaves stripped and chopped fine

1   Preheat the oven to 175 degrees F. Arrange the tomatoes in a single layer on a baking sheet, leaving space around the edges. Using a pastry brush, brush the tops with a light coating of olive oil. You may also drizzle a small amount of olive oil over, just be sure to go lightly. Sprinkle the tomatoes lightly with salt—the liquid will evaporate from the tomatoes and concentrate the salt over time. Sprinkle the tomatoes with chopped thyme, going light or heavy, as you like.

2   Roast in the oven until the tomatoes are dehydrated and chewy, like tomato candy, anywhere from 3 to 6 hours. They should not brown, so check periodically while roasting and lower the temperature if needed.

MORE GARDEN RECIPES: Tomato chips can be chopped and added to mayonnaise for a flavorful condiment. I like them folded into soft-scrambled eggs and as a layer in sandwiches.

Herby Pasta with Lettuce and Prosciutto

This recipe was one of those happy accidental creations that I made one day. I didn't have much in the pantry, and I started just throwing ingredients into a pan. I left onions and prosciutto to sit and get crispy, then doused them with some pasta water to make a thick broth. At the last minute, I added handfuls of lettuce to the pot—a great way to incorporate greens into a pasta dish. Use whatever greens you have on hand—Bibb lettuce, romaine, radicchio, arugula, parsley, mint, basil, lovage, and so on. This is also a great way to use up any lettuce that may be starting to bolt and turn bitter or may have begun to wilt with age. Choose a shaped pasta (bowtie is my favorite), not a long noodle.

SERVES 4

- 3 tablespoons olive oil
- 1 tablespoon butter
- 5 garlic cloves, peeled and sliced
- 1 shallot, chopped
- 4 slices prosciutto, torn into pieces
- 1 tablespoon dry vermouth
- 4 cups bowtie or other shaped pasta
- 4 cups mixed lettuce greens
- ½ cup mixed herbs
- Parmesan for garnish (optional)

1 Boil a pot of salted water for the pasta.

2 In large sauté pan with high sides, heat the olive oil and butter over medium-high heat. When the butter is melted and starting to bubble, add the garlic and shallot. Sauté until cooked and starting to brown at the edges, 8 to 10 minutes. Add the

prosciutto and let sit, stirring only occasionally, allowing it to get brown and crispy, about 4 minutes. When the mixture starts to stick to the bottom of the pan, deglaze with the vermouth and scrape up any brown bits. Cook the vermouth down for 1 minute, then remove the pan from the heat.

3   Drop the pasta into the boiling water and cook until just al dente, about 10 minutes for bowtie pasta. A minute before the pasta is ready, put the sauté pan back over high heat. It will start to sizzle almost immediately. Pour a cup of the pasta water into the sauté pan and stir continuously.

4   When the pasta is al dente, drain and add to the sauté pan. Cook until the pasta water starts to evaporate and bubble at the bottom of the pan, about 3 minutes. Add the greens and herbs, one handful at a time, and toss to wilt. Continue adding until all are incorporated, then immediately remove from the heat. Spoon four equal portions into shallow bowls; if using, shave Parmesan over the top and serve immediately.

MORE GARDEN RECIPES: Homegrown lettuces make wonderful salads, of course. Dress simply with olive oil, lemon juice, salt, and freshly ground black pepper. Lettuces can also be used to make a lettuce soup—sauté onions until cooked, add lettuce, add stock, and purée with some cream.

Pea Falafel

Falafel is traditionally made with mashed chickpeas; this version also uses garden peas. The peas lend the falafel a fresh, verdant taste and are perfect for using up an apartment garden harvest. Try the falafel wrapped up in the Salt and Nigella Flatbread (page 119) and served with some pickled cucumbers and a spoonful of yogurt.

SERVES 4

- 1¼ cups dried chickpeas
- 1¼ cups shelled peas
- ½ large onion, chopped
- ¼ cup chickpea flour
- ½ teaspoon baking soda
- 1 teaspoon kosher salt
- 1 teaspoon smoked paprika
- 1 teaspoon curry powder
- 1 teaspoon garam masala
- ¼ teaspoon freshly ground black pepper
- ¼ teaspoon cayenne
- 1 cup fresh herbs, such as lemon balm, mint, anise hyssop, lovage, tarragon, parsley, cilantro
- ½ lemon, zested and juiced
- Olive oil for frying

1   The night before, soak the chickpeas on the counter in a bowl of cool water. Drain well in the morning and pat dry if still wet.

2   Bring a pot of salted water to a boil. Set up an ice-water bath, filling a large bowl with cold water and ice. Set aside. Drop the shelled peas into the boiling water and cook until bright green and floating, 2 to 3 minutes. Drain and immediately drop them into the ice-water bath, halting the cooking process. Give them a stir to make sure they are cool, then drain and set aside.

3   Place the soaked chickpeas and peas in the bowl of a food processor fitted with a steel blade. Add all the remaining ingredients except the olive oil. Blend until broken down and well combined. The batter will be almost pastelike and should hold together. If it's too wet, add another spoonful of chickpea flour. Scrape it out of the processor bowl into another bowl and let stand for 30 minutes.

4   In a large sauté pan, add enough olive oil to cover the bottom of the pan and come up the sides a bit. Heat over medium heat. When the oil is hot, drop in small spoonfuls of the falafel batter and fry. The batter is quite soft, so do not move the cooking falafels around. Let the frying side get nice and golden brown before flipping them over. Continue frying on all sides until golden brown. Remove from the pan and drain on a paper bag. Repeat with the remaining batter. Serve immediately.

MORE GARDEN RECIPES: Peas make a great filling; you can mash them to fill ravioli or savory tarts. Try replacing half of the ricotta in the filling for the Borage Zucchini Tart (page 149) with mashed peas. Whole peas are also wonderful served with long pasta noodles. Make a quick sauce with prosciutto and butter in a sauté pan, add the peas, then toss with pasta. Finish with fresh mint and a grate or two of lemon zest.

LEMON
VERBENA

SCENTED
GERANIUM

NASTURTIUM

CHIVE
BLOSSOMS

THYME

BORAGE

MARIGOLD

Edible Blossoms

Many plants produce flowers that are edible, often with a more muted version of the plant's leaf, stem, or root flavor. These blossoms can be harvested and eaten as well! They make a pretty presentation, and it's a good way to use all of the plant before pruning after bloom.

ANISE HYSSOP: Gentle licorice flavor. Flower heads form a spike of many individual blossoms. To harvest, close one fist around the flower spike and with your other hand pull the stem down to strip off the blossoms.

ARUGULA: Flouncy white petals that taste of spicy pepper and are a bit nutty.

BORAGE: Beautiful blue-violet flowers that taste mildly of cucumber.

CHAMOMILE: Sweet, floral flavor. Best used in teas or cooked.

CHERVIL: Feathery white blossoms that taste slightly of fennel.

CHIVE: Spiky purple flowers that taste strongly of onion.

DANDELION: Bright yellow petals that taste rich and buttery.

MARJORAM: Similar to oregano, these tiny flowers are best as garnish.

NASTURTIUM: Slightly peppery and brightly colored, these are great in salad.

SCENTED GERANIUM: Tastes like the plant variety's particular scent and is wonderful candied for garnish.

SQUASH: These big orange flowers don't taste like much, but their size makes them perfect for stuffing and cooking. Make sure you harvest only male blossoms (with a stamen—trust me, it should be obvious) and leave the female blossoms to produce fruit.

THYME: Tiny little flowers with a strong thyme flavor.

Thyme-Roasted Chicken Legs
with Charred Onions

Inevitably, if I roast a chicken, the first piece I grab is the leg. It is often the case that I miss out, if I'm being polite to guests and letting them choose first. My friend Michelle solves this conundrum in her own family by purchasing an extra package of legs every time she roasts a chicken. Brilliant! Thyme is liberally added to both the chicken and onions in this recipe, but truly the beauty lies in the roasting. The chicken is started at a very high temperature. After twenty minutes, the legs are cooked slowly at a lower temperature for nearly an hour and come out of the oven almost like a confit—crispy outside, succulent inside. The result is a simple but homey dish of sweet onions and crispy chicken. As thyme is a hardy herb, this dish can be made well into the winter with thyme from the garden.

SERVES 4

- 8 chicken legs
- Kosher salt
- 2 onions, peeled and cut into half-moons or rings of medium thickness
- 3 tablespoons olive oil
- 6 tablespoons chopped thyme, divided, plus more for garnish
- ½ teaspoon freshly ground black pepper
- 1 lemon, zested

1   Prepare the chicken legs by salting liberally at least an hour before cooking, and up to a day ahead. Store in a resealable plastic bag or plastic wrap and refrigerate until ready to use.

2   Preheat the oven to 450 degrees F. In a large bowl, combine the onions, olive oil, and 3 tablespoons of the thyme and toss to coat. Spread the onions in an even layer on a large sheet pan. In the same bowl, combine the remaining thyme, 1 teaspoon salt, pepper, lemon zest, and the chicken legs. Toss to coat, rubbing some of the seasoning under the skin of the legs. Lay the legs directly on top of the onions, making sure the legs don't touch each other or overlap.

3   Put the sheet pan in the oven and roast for 20 minutes. Without opening the oven door, reduce the heat to 350 degrees F and bake for an additional 45 minutes to 1 hour, or until the legs are golden brown and wrinkled. Check the pan every 15 minutes; if the onions along the edges are turning too black, toss as needed.

4   Remove the pan from the oven and transfer the onions to a large platter. Set the legs on top of the onions and garnish with a pinch of fresh thyme if desired. Serve immediately.

MORE GARDEN RECIPES: Thyme is a great partner to lemon. Steep a sprig of thyme in lemonade or make a hot tea of thyme and lemon slices with honey. You can also make just the onions from this dish and bake them on a square of puff pastry for a quick party appetizer. Thyme infuses well; try substituting thyme for the anise hyssop in the Anise Hyssop Ice Cream (page 159) and serve with a bowl of berries.

RECIPES FROM THE GARDEN

Seared Pork Chops
with Fig-Lovage Relish

I love figs, and I have long been a fan of lovage, which deserves to be much more widely known. Lovage tastes like a stronger version of a celery leaf. As its flavor is more pronounced, a little goes a long way. I serve this relish with seared pork chops, but it would be great on most roasted meats or a fatty fish like black cod. The pork chops are lightly rubbed with fennel seeds, crushed coriander seeds, and paprika. It's a nice smoky combination of flavors to play off the sweetness of the figs. Feel free to omit the rub entirely and simply season the pork with salt and pepper; it will be equally delicious.

SERVES 4

Relish

- 12 dried figs, Calimyrna or Black Mission
- 4 tablespoons finely chopped lovage (about 12 large leaves)
- 1 teaspoon sherry vinegar
- 1 tablespoon olive oil

Rub

- 1 tablespoon fennel seed, ground
- ½ teaspoon freshly ground coriander
- ½ teaspoon kosher salt
- ½ teaspoon freshly ground black pepper

Pork Chops

- 2 tablespoons olive oil
- ½ tablespoon butter
- 4 pork chops, rib chop, bone-in
- 1 tablespoon vermouth →

1   To make the relish, chop the figs into small dice. Add the lovage, sherry vinegar, and olive oil. Stir and set aside to macerate.

2   To make the rub, combine the fennel, coriander, salt, and pepper. Sprinkle the rub on both sides of each of the chops and pat it in. You want a pretty thin sprinkling, not a thick layer, so use sparingly, but use it all.

3   To prepare the pork chops, heat the olive oil and butter in a large sauté pan over medium heat. When the butter is melted and bubbling at the edges and the pan is hot, add the pork chops. Let sear until golden brown. Don't move the chops around; let them just sit and color. After about 6 minutes, you can see that the sides of the chops are beginning to cook. Flip them over and cook until cooked through and firm, another 5 to 6 minutes. Transfer the chops to a plate and let them rest. Return the pan to the stovetop and increase the heat to high. The brown bits in the pan will start to sizzle and burn. Splash in the vermouth and quickly scrape loose all the bits. Cook for 1 minute more, then remove from heat.

4   To serve, place one pork chop per person on a dinner plate and garnish with a spoonful of the relish. Distribute pan juices evenly over the chops and serve immediately.

MORE GARDEN RECIPES: Lovage is a natural accompaniment to shellfish. Steam a big pot of clams or mussels and add lovage when you add the shellfish. Lovage is also wonderful with eggs; for a healthy breakfast, soft-boil an egg and mash it onto a piece of toast, then garnish with a chopped lovage leaf and salt.

Lemon Trout
with Dandelion Greens

Whole fish can sometimes be intimidating, but trout cooks quickly and tastes great. No need to clean anything—commercial trout comes already scaled and gutted. I learned this wholesome and healthy recipe from my friend Jaime years ago; it has been a standard of mine ever since. Whole trout is cooked quickly under the broiler and served topped with a salad of dandelion greens and almonds. The dandelion greens are quite bitter, but work well with the subtle fish. They are also very healthy for you; ounce for ounce, they have more vitamin A, iron, and calcium than broccoli. Harvest new dandelion growth in spring; older, bigger leaves are too tough and woody, and their flavor is harsh.

SERVES 2

- 1 garlic clove, peeled
- 1 handful sliced almonds
- 2 handfuls dandelion greens, coarsely chopped
- 1 lemon, zested, then sliced
- 1 tablespoon olive oil
- Kosher salt
- 1 whole trout
- Freshly ground black pepper

1   Preheat the broiler, first raising a rack to the highest position in the oven.

2   In the bowl of a mortar and pestle, mash and grind the garlic clove. When the oils have covered the walls of the mortar, remove and discard the garlic flesh. Add the almonds to the bowl and grind until they are broken up into smaller pieces. Add the dandelion greens and lemon zest and mash all the →

ingredients together until combined. The mixture will look a little bit like a salad and a little bit like a pesto. Inconsistency in the size of the leafy bits is perfect. Add the olive oil and a pinch of salt and give it one last stir with the pestle. Set aside.

3   Meanwhile, season the trout on both sides and inside the belly with salt and pepper. Insert several lemon slices into the belly of the trout. Place on a sheet pan and lightly coat the trout with a drizzle of olive oil to prevent sticking. Place the sheet pan directly under the broiler, and broil on one side until the skin starts to shrivel and char, 4 to 5 minutes. Take out the pan and flip the trout with a spatula. Return to the broiler and broil the other side until charred and cooked through, 4 to 5 minutes.

4   Place the broiled trout on a platter and spoon the dandelion salad over it. Serve immediately.

MORE GARDEN RECIPES: Dandelions are a great green for adding to your salad, but use them sparingly so they don't overpower the other flavors. Try making a dandelion pesto with crushed garlic and pine nuts. Dandelion greens can also be used as a filling for the Pea Vine Dumplings (page 121).

Borage Zucchini Tart

This tart is made in stages, but it's worth the extra time. Using store-bought puff pastry, the tart is layered with borage-scented ricotta cheese and sautéed zucchini, then topped with a lattice of zucchini slices. Latticework takes time, so if you prefer not to fuss with it, simply layer zucchini in a row across the tart. Borage has a very distinct cucumber-like flavor and pairs nicely with zucchini. It's a great way to make use of a prolific container plant. If you are so inclined, you can make just the borage-ricotta mixture and serve a big spoonful over some pasta dressed in olive oil. The cheese may also be used on crostini as an appetizer or as filling in homemade ravioli. The tart can be made a day ahead, wrapped loosely in parchment paper and refrigerated until ready to serve.

SERVES 4

- Flour for dusting
- 1 sheet puff pastry
- 2 large zucchini
- 1 tablespoon butter
- 1 tablespoon olive oil
- ½ onion, finely chopped
- Kosher salt
- 1 cup ricotta

- 30 borage leaves, finely chopped
- 1 lemon, zested
- 2 tablespoons grated Parmesan
- ½ teaspoon freshly ground black pepper
- 1 egg yolk, beaten →

1   To prepare the pastry shell, lightly dust a countertop with flour and roll out the puff pastry dough until it is half its original thickness—about an 11-by-11-inch square. Make three folds along each side of the dough, ¼-inch wide, folding toward the center of the dough to form a rim of puff pastry. This rim will contain the filling. Press together firmly at the corners. Don't worry if your pastry isn't a perfect square; the dough will puff up in baking and these little imperfections will not show. Move the tart shell to a sheet pan and freeze until ready to use.

2   For the lattice top, slice one zucchini lengthwise on the thinnest setting of a mandoline, or using a knife, cut lengthwise into very thin strips. Set the strips on a cooling rack set over a sheet pan and salt lightly; this helps extract some moisture from the zucchini.

3   While the zucchini strips are draining, chop the remaining zucchini into small, even dice. Heat the butter and olive oil in a large sauté pan over medium-high heat. When the butter is melted, add the onions and cook until soft and translucent, 8 to 10 minutes. Add the diced zucchini and a pinch of salt and sauté until the zucchini is just cooked through, about 4 minutes. Remove from the heat and spread the mixture on a sheet pan in a thin layer to cool.

4   In a small bowl, stir together the ricotta, borage, lemon zest, Parmesan, and pepper until well combined.

5   Press the zucchini strips between layers of kitchen towels or paper towels to remove any remaining excess moisture.

6   Preheat the oven to 375 degrees F.

7   To assemble the tart, take the pastry shell from the freezer. Spread the ricotta mixture over the bottom of the shell. Evenly distribute the sautéed zucchini-onion mixture over the ricotta. Lay the zucchini slices across the tart, from top to bottom, overlapping the layers slightly. Working perpendicular to this layer, lay zucchini slices left to right. Make a latticework pattern by lifting every other row of zucchini running top to bottom and tucking the new horizontal slices over and under. Weave the strips across the entire tart, tucking under or cutting the edges so they do not hang over the tart walls.

8   When the lattice is complete, brush the entire top of the tart with the egg yolk. Bake until puffed up and golden brown, 40 to 45 minutes. Serve hot or at room temperature.

MORE GARDEN RECIPES: Borage flowers make a lovely garnish for cocktails and summertime drinks. Young borage leaves can be torn and added to salads, imparting a soft cucumber flavor. For a light summer salad, sliver borage leaves and toss them with some steamed shrimp, lemon juice, and avocado.

Stuffed Peppers

I am a one-trick pony with my stuffing or filling ingredients, but that's because this recipe is so delicious and works with pretty much any veg. Here, I cut peppers of any size in half, remove the seeds, and fill them with a simple but memorable stuffing of caramelized vegetables, fresh herbs, and pine nuts. Works like a charm!

SERVES 2

- ¼ cup extra virgin olive oil, plus more for baking
- 1 medium yellow onion, finely diced
- 1 medium carrot, peeled and finely diced
- 1 garlic clove, minced
- ½ cup bread crumbs
- ¼ cup pine nuts, chopped
- ¼ cup currants or dried fruit, finely chopped
- 2 tablespoons finely chopped thyme
- ½ teaspoon smoked paprika
- 1 lemon, zested, then sliced
- 6 small peppers, such as cherry bomb or Anaheim, cut in half
- Kosher salt
- Freshly ground black pepper

1. Preheat the oven to 375 degrees F.

2. In a medium frying pan, add the olive oil and set over medium heat. Once warmed, add the onion and cook, stirring occasionally, until onions are soft and translucent, 8 to 10 minutes. Add the carrots and cook until soft and browning around the edges, another 6 to 8 minutes. Add the garlic and cook until all the vegetables are caramelized and starting to stick to the pan. You don't want them charred; you're going for →

a slower-cooked, caramelized vegetable. Add the bread crumbs, pine nuts, currants, and thyme and stir occasionally until slightly toasted, about 4 minutes more. The bread crumbs will absorb the oil. Keep stirring until everything is well incorporated. If the bread crumbs look dry, add a small spoonful of olive oil.

3   Remove the pan from heat and add the smoked paprika and lemon zest, salt and pepper to taste, stirring to combine. Place the pepper halves, cut side up, in a medium-sized baking dish. Fill each pepper with a few spoonfuls of the mixture, pressing down to fill.

4   Drizzle the peppers with olive oil and bake until the peppers are soft and beginning to char along the edges, 35 to 40 minutes.

5   Remove the baking dish from the oven and let the stuffed peppers cool slightly before serving.

MORE GARDEN RECIPES: All sorts of vegetables can be stuffed in this way. You can hollow out the seeds from a zucchini or scoop out a tomato. Simple olive-basted roasted peppers are both delicious and easy.

Chamomile and Coconut Granola

My friend Lynda makes the most delicious granola, and so naturally, I stole her recipe. This isn't a typical granola with butter and sugar—it's a toasted combination of flaky coconut, oats, and almonds. The flavor is intensified with some chamomile buds and sesame seeds. Serve by the handful over a bowl of plain yogurt with a drizzle of honey and some fresh fruit. Super yummy and super healthy.

MAKES 6 SERVINGS

- 1 cup rolled oats
- 1 cup sliced almonds
- 1 cup raw, unsweetened coconut flakes
- 1 tablespoon untoasted sesame seeds
- 1 tablespoon flaxseed meal
- 1 teaspoon crushed dried chamomile buds
- ¼ teaspoon kosher salt

Preheat the oven to 350 degrees F. Place all the ingredients on a sheet pan and stir to combine. Toast in the oven for 5 minutes. Remove the pan from the oven and toss, redistributing the granola but keeping it in a single layer. Toast for another 3 to 4 minutes, or until the coconut flakes are golden brown. Cooled leftover granola can be stored in a sealed container at room temperature for about 3 weeks.

MORE GARDEN RECIPES: Chamomile is a great fit with oats. Try some in your oatmeal, add some to your favorite oatmeal cookie recipe, or toss some crushed buds into a topping for fruit crisp.

Rosy Strawberries
with Buttermilk Cake

Rose geranium is an easy-to-grow flower (see page 75) that is best used in sweet recipes and desserts. It imparts a distinctive flavor to a dish, and I love its floral scent with strawberries. In this recipe, ripe berries are simply macerated with some sugar and finely chopped rose geranium leaves. On the side, I like to serve this easy buttermilk cake. The sweet rosy sauce can also be eaten spooned over vanilla ice cream, or on its own, maybe with a splash of cream on top.

SERVES 4

Strawberries

- 1 pint strawberries, hulled and quartered
- ¼ cup sugar
- 5 large rose geranium leaves, chopped fine

Cake

- 1 cup whole wheat pastry flour
- 1 cup all-purpose flour
- 1 teaspoon baking powder
- 1 teaspoon baking soda
- ½ teaspoon kosher salt
- 1 cup buttermilk
- 1 teaspoon vanilla extract
- ½ cup (1 stick) unsalted butter, at room temperature
- 1 cup sugar
- 2 large eggs
- Powdered sugar (optional) →

1   Combine the strawberries, sugar, and rose geranium leaves in a small bowl and let stand for 30 minutes before serving.

2   Preheat the oven to 350 degrees F. Butter a 9-inch cake pan and set aside. Combine the flours, baking powder, baking soda, and salt in a small bowl and set aside. Combine the buttermilk and vanilla in a separate bowl and set aside.

3   Using an electric mixer, cream the butter and sugar until well incorporated, about 5 minutes. The mixture should be light and fluffy. Add the eggs, one at a time, mixing until well incorporated, scraping the sides of the bowl. Add half of the flour mixture and stir until just combined. Add the buttermilk mixture and stir until well combined. Add the remainder of the flour mixture and stir until just combined. Pour the batter into the cake pan and bake for 30 to 40 minutes, or until a toothpick inserted in the middle comes out clean.

4   Cool the cake on a cooling rack and dust with powdered sugar, if desired. Serve with a generous spoonful of macerated berries.

MORE GARDEN RECIPES: Rose geranium can be steeped in cream for an ice cream base or a scented whipped cream. Try blending leaves with milk and strawberries for a quick, nutritious breakfast smoothie.

Anise Hyssop Ice Cream

I fell in love with the conical shape of the purple anise hyssop flower at a farmers' market years ago. Taking a bite, I fell in love a second time—with the flavor. Having no idea what to do with this new herb—part licorice, kind of minty—I steeped it in some milk and made ice cream. It quickly became one of my favorites; I make this often, pairing it with berries and cakes instead of the usual suspect, vanilla.

MAKES ABOUT 2 PINTS

- 1½ cups whole milk
- ½ cup sugar
- 10 anise hyssop leaves
- 3 egg yolks, plus 1 whole egg
- 1½ cups heavy cream

1. In a medium saucepan, heat the milk, sugar, and anise hyssop leaves over medium heat until hot but not boiling. Remove from the heat and let steep for about 30 minutes, or until the flavor tastes good to you. Return the mixture to medium heat and warm through.

2. In a glass bowl, whisk the egg yolks and egg until well combined. Add one ladleful of the warm milk mixture to the eggs, whisking continuously. Add another ladleful and whisk until well combined. (You are tempering the eggs slowly to a warm liquid so that you do not cook them when you add them to the saucepan.)

3. Pour the egg mixture into the saucepan with the milk mixture and cook over medium heat, stirring continuously, for about 8 minutes. Be careful not to boil. Cook, stirring often, until →

the custard lightly coats the back of a wooden spoon. Remove the custard from the heat and strain into a large mixing bowl. (Straining will remove any curdled egg as well as the anise hyssop leaves.) Add the heavy cream and stir to combine.

4   Lay plastic wrap directly on the surface of the custard and refrigerate until cold, at least 4 hours or overnight. Freeze according to the manufacturer's instructions in an ice cream maker, occasionally scraping the sides of the bowl, until creamy and frozen. Store the ice cream in an airtight container in the freezer until ready to serve.

MORE GARDEN RECIPES: Add a few anise hyssop leaves to a grain or legume salad for a fresh flavor combination. Anise hyssop is also wonderful in herbal sun teas.

Berry Apple Crisp with Lovage

Lovage is an herb typically used in savory recipes, but the aromatic seeds also work in sweet desserts. Baked fruit crisps are one of the simplest and quickest desserts to make. The combination of apples and berries, along with the lovage seeds, makes this a perfect seasonal dessert to serve in late summer. Serve the crisp with ice cream or whipped cream on the side. Any leftovers can be refrigerated or covered tightly in parchment paper and held at room temperature.

SERVES 4 TO 6

Filling

- 1½ pounds apples, cut into large chunks
- 1½ pounds mixed berries, such as blueberries and blackberries
- 1 cup sugar

Topping

- ½ cup whole wheat pastry flour
- ½ cup rolled oats
- ½ cup brown sugar
- ¼ cup coarsely chopped pecans
- 1½ teaspoons ground cinnamon
- 1 teaspoon lovage seeds, gently crushed
- ¼ teaspoon freshly grated nutmeg
- ¼ teaspoon kosher salt
- 6 tablespoons unsalted butter, chilled

1   Preheat the oven to 350 degrees F, first setting a rack in the center.

2   In a large bowl, toss the apples, berries, and sugar. Pour into a large baking dish and set aside.

3   To make the topping, combine the flour, oats, brown sugar, pecans, cinnamon, lovage, nutmeg, salt, and butter. Using your fingertips, massage the mixture together until it forms a coarse crumb and larger clumps. Spread evenly over the fruit.

4   Bake on the center rack until the topping is golden brown and juices bubble around the sides, 40 to 45 minutes.

MORE GARDEN RECIPES: Lovage seeds are a great spice for your cupboard. You can grind lovage and use is as a rub for grilled or roasted meats. Lovage can take the place of fennel seeds in most recipes.

Blackberry Buttermilk Ice Cream

This blackberry buttermilk ice cream is nearly guilt free, as it uses low-fat buttermilk and a minimum of sugar. Be sure to rinse off city-picked blackberries before you use them. I learned how to adjust the freezing temperature of ice cream years ago from my chef friend Thierry. He makes killer sorbets, and I could never figure out how he did it. Turns out a bit of booze raises the freezing temperature of the mix and therefore makes it seem a bit smoother and less icy. A good tip to keep in your pocket.

MAKES 1 PINT

- ½ pound blackberries (about 2 cups)
- ¼ cup sugar
- 1 cup low-fat buttermilk
- 1 teaspoon vodka

1   In a bowl, macerate the blackberries and sugar for 30 minutes on your countertop. When juicy, purée in a blender with the buttermilk and vodka. Pour through a fine mesh sieve to strain out all the blackberry seeds and hairs.

2   Add the mixture to an ice cream maker and freeze according to the manufacturer's instructions, occasionally scraping the sides of the bowl, until creamy and frozen. Store the ice cream in an airtight container in the freezer until ready to serve.

MORE GARDEN RECIPES: Try the Berry Apple Crisp (see page 162) or jam for more blackberry ideas.

Lemon Verbena Ice

In the heat of summer, there's nothing like an icy, refreshing sweet treat or beverage. Lemon verbena is at its best in midsummer—this plant loves the heat. It also tends to be prolific and will put on growth quickly once it is cut. This recipe is quite simple and can be used with a number of different herbs. It is essentially an infused simple syrup, frozen with a bit of wine. To make an icy granita, you must rake through the mixture as it freezes every 15 minutes or so to separate the crystals. This results in a very icy dessert, not nearly as smooth as a sorbet. You can also use the granita in beverages. Scoop some into a glass and splash with some gin and fizzy soda for an evening cocktail. Add some fresh lemon verbena leaves as garnish.

SERVES 4 TO 6

- 2 cups water
- 2 cups sugar
- 20 to 30 lemon verbena leaves
- 1 cup light, crisp white wine, such as Sauvignon Blanc
- 1 tablespoon lemon juice

In a medium saucepan, bring the water, sugar, and lemon verbena leaves to a boil. Stir to dissolve the sugar, then remove from the heat and let steep. When the mixture has cooled, taste to make sure the lemon verbena flavor is nice and strong. If not, add a fresh round of leaves, bring to a boil, and steep some more. When the flavor is right, add the wine, then strain out the leaves and pour the liquid into a shallow baking dish. Freeze for 20 minutes, then check to see whether the liquid is partially frozen. Pull a fork through frozen sections to loosen and break up the crystals, and return to the freezer. Wait 15 minutes and repeat. Continue doing this until the entire mixture is flaky and frozen.

MORE GARDEN RECIPES: Lemon verbena is commonly used in teas and is delicious steeped on its own with honey. Its leaves may be steeped in cream for ice cream or custards. This herb also pairs nicely with lamb and game meats. Add chopped leaves to marinades for lamb chops or steaks. Lemon verbena can also be used as a substitute for lemon zest in some recipes.

Sugar Petals

I find that while some edible flowers are flavorful, most petals don't taste like much of anything. When I have a plant that produces flowers and I want to fancy up desserts or platters of fruit, I make sugared petals and use them as small garnishes. You can employ this same method with herb leaves. Sugared mint, anise hyssop, and even sage are delicious touches that are not only flavorful but lovely to look at.

It is quite easy, but tedious work to sugar petals and leaves, so be ready to practice your patience! Prepare your space. Set up a cooling rack on a sheet pan. The cooling rack will be used to dry the petals once they're sugared. The sheet pan will collect all of the excess sugar. You'll also need tweezers and a pastry brush or small paintbrush.

Cut flower stems from the plant and gently break apart the flower head to release individual petals. In a small bowl, beat one egg white, then thin with a splash of water. Pick up each petal with the tweezers (so your fingers don't stick to the petal). Brush the petal with a thin coat of egg wash. For large leaves, you can lay them in the palm of your hand when brushing. Be sure to coat both sides. (And no, you can't get lazy and just dip the leaf or petal—the coating will be far too thick.) When both sides are brushed with the egg white wash, hold the leaf or petal with the tweezers and sprinkle sugar on each side, holding it over the sheet pan so any excess sugar can be reused. Set on the cooling rack to dry.

Here is a short list of pretty petals and flavorful leaves to sugar:

- Anise hyssop leaves
- Lemon verbena
- Mint leaves
- Nasturtium
- Rose geranium

Water-Bath Canning 101

This is a step-by-step guide to water-bath canning at home. There are a few options to choose from, but all work well. Be sure to set up your jars and workspace beforehand so you can establish a rhythm. Also, be mindful of the processing times given in recipes.

CLEANING THE JARS: Wash the jars and lids in hot soapy water and set them to dry completely on a rack or a clean dish towel.

PREPARING THE JARS: Glass jars and lids do not need to be sterilized before use if your foodstuffs will be processed for more than 10 minutes in a boiling water bath or pressure canner. If jar-processing time is 10 minutes or less, jars must be sterilized before filling. Do this by placing the jars in a canning pot, filling with water, and bringing the water to a simmer. Hold the jars in water until you're ready to fill.

FILLING THE JARS: All canned goods will need headspace to allow for expansion of the food and to create a vacuum in cooling jars. As a general rule, leave ¼ inch of headspace on all jams and jellies and ½ inch of headspace on all whole fruits and vegetables, like with pickles. When using whole fruits and vegetables, release air bubbles in just-filled jars by tapping the jar on the counter or inserting a wooden chopstick or skewer into the jar and gently stirring the fruit. When placing lids and rings on canning jars, do not overtighten the rings. Secure just until the rings have tension and feel snug. Overtightening will not allow air to vent from the jars—a crucial step in canning.

HEATING THE CANNING POT: Fill your canning pot or a deep stockpot half full of water and heat to a low boil. Hold the liquid on a very low boil until ready to use.

FILLING THE CANNING POT: If using a canning pot, place the prepared jars of food on the rack in the canner. Do not stack, as you need to allow for circulation of water for proper sealing.

Lower the jars into the canning pot and add enough water to cover the jar tops by an inch or more. Cover the pot and return to a boil. *Processing times begin once the canning-pot water is brought back up to a boil.* This can take as long as 15 minutes, so be sure to keep an eye on your pot and a timer nearby. You may also use a deep stockpot (best only in small-batch preserving) by lining the bottom of the pot with a dish towel and placing jars on top. This helps keep jars from clanging around on the bottom of the pot or tumbling over onto their sides. This form of canning is not universally recommended or endorsed by the USDA, but I have seen plenty of farmers and European country folk use this old-school technique, and I've adapted their laissez-faire ways.

REMOVING SEALED JARS: Using a jar lifter or a set of kitchen tongs, remove jars from the canner when the processing time has elapsed. (Remember, processing times begin once the canning-pot water is brought back up to a boil.) Set the jars aside on a folded towel to cool. Make sure you *do not press* on the tops and create an artificial seal.

KNOWING WHEN JARS ARE SEALED: You'll hear the sound of can tops popping shortly—a sign that a secure seal has been made. Once the jars are cool, check the seal by removing the outer ring and lifting the jar by holding only the lid. If it stays intact, you have successfully canned your food. If the seal is loose or broken, you can reprocess in the water bath within twenty-four hours. Be sure to use a new lid, and check the jar rim for cracks or nicks and replace if necessary. Or you can refrigerate the jar immediately and use within three weeks.

LABELING AND STORAGE: Once cool, label all jars with date and contents. Successfully sealed jars should be stored in a cool, dark place such as a cupboard. Officially, canned goods keep for up to a year, but I have let them go a bit longer with little effect.

Windowsill and Countertop Projects

Let's face it: gardening isn't for everyone. Even if you're interested in growing food at home, if you have a crazy schedule or you really don't want to be responsible for tending to something on a daily basis, gardening may not be for you. Or it could be that your space is not conducive to gardening. Some yards and patios get so little sun that an urbanite's only hope for farm-fresh produce is a weekly visit to the farmers' market. That is OK. No sense in trying to jam a square peg into a round hole. There are lots of other options for you that are super simple. They may not fill up dinner plate after dinner plate, but they will add small, fresh touches to your meals and help you feel like you're growing *something* green.

MICROGREENS

Microgreens are all the rage with chefs, and you've likely eaten them without even knowing it. Teeny tiny plants that are only two to three weeks old and have only two true sets of leaves are considered microgreens. These little plants are easily identified by taste—they pack a flavorful punch. Many vegetables make tasty microgreens that can be used as garnish on dishes. You don't want to cook these; the flavor is too delicate to withstand heat. But they're great as a finishing flavor accent for your meals, sprinkled over seared fish or grilled meat. What's more, microgreens are ready to eat in just a few weeks. This short time frame fits the needs of many busy urbanites. Microgreens need very little attention and can be grown right in a baking dish on your windowsill. As you are not going to be concerned about the overall health of the plants, even with limited natural light you need not worry about feeding them. You barely even need to water microgreens. Just keep a spray bottle handy and keep the seeds moist until they germinate.

How to Start a Microgreen Garden

Fill a shallow tray with seed-starting mix (page 85). Don't underfill the tray—add enough mix so it is flush with the top. You can use a plastic garden tray, like you find at nurseries and hardware stores, or use what you have—a shallow baking dish or roasting pan will work. Broadcast the seeds densely across the surface of the mix. Spray with a water bottle to saturate the surface. Cover with plastic wrap to hold in moisture and create some heat. Place in a windowsill or a spot that receives good light. To speed up the process, you can use grow lights. Keep the mix moist and lift the wrap to ventilate the dish every day or two. In just a few days you will see green sprouts pushing out of the growing medium. Wait until they reach one to two inches tall and have two true leaves (these look more like what the plant's leaves look like when mature, and are different from the first two leaves found on sprouts) to harvest. Cut as close to the seed mix as possible. When you've harvested the whole tray, start again. You should be able to use the same seed-starting medium two or three times before having to refresh. If it ever grows moldy from excess moisture, toss it out and replenish with fresh seed-starting mix.

Seeds for Microgreens

- Arugula
- Basil
- Beets
- Celery
- Cilantro
- Cucumber
- Parsley
- Radish
- Sorrel

Sprouts

You likely think of sprouts as those dense and wiry, tasteless greens that people insist on using on vegetable sandwiches. There was a time when you couldn't eat at a deli without seeing the ubiquitous vegetarian sandwich offering: cream cheese, cucumber, and alfalfa sprouts. (Did I just date myself?) Sprouts, however, can be delicious, and are now thought to be a super food—more on that shortly. Lately, they've cropped up more and more in restaurants and in groceries, where you can find them in the refrigerated section with fresh foods.

Sprouts are essentially the very first growth a seed puts out before it develops true leaves. Mung bean sprouts are a great example of what a sprout looks and tastes like. Sprouts add a fresh crispy texture to dishes and are packed with nutrients. Seeds store all the energy and food needed to produce healthy plants. By eating them at a very early stage of growth, we reap the rewards of all that good energy.

Different sprouts will carry different flavors, of course. Legumes like peas or mung beans produce thick, crunchy sprouts. Broccoli and alfalfa sprouts are more delicate and won't have as much flavor. Alliums like onions and scallions are a bit slimy feeling, but they have a good strong onion taste. Play around a bit and see what you like.

Be sure to choose seed that is clean and organic. The directions I offer include a disinfecting process, but I will skip this step when I know I'm using a clean seed source. It's up to you, but this recipe is a safe version that can be used on any seed.

Sprouts are, by far, some of the easiest things to "grow" at home. No soil and no windowsill required, and the entire process →

takes anywhere from three to five days. You need only a quart-size glass jar to get going. Basically, you give seeds a moist environment and rinse them every few hours. Some sources say to cover the jar on your counter to avoid photosynthesis so the sprout doesn't develop a leaf, while some say it doesn't matter. I've done it both ways with success, but I tend to cover the jar. If I want small greens, I plant seeds as a microgreen (page 173) instead.

MATERIALS

- 1 teaspoon bleach
- Water
- One large jar
- ¼ cup seeds
- Small length of cheesecloth

DIRECTIONS

1   Disinfect the seeds (a necessary step, as some may carry *E. coli*). Combine the bleach with 1 cup of tap water in a small mixing bowl. Add the seeds and soak for 15 minutes. Drain and rinse thoroughly three times.

2   Place the clean seed in the bottom of the jar.

3   Fill the jar with 1 cup of water.

4   Cover the jar with a double layer of cheesecloth and secure with a rubber band. This allows for air circulation.

5   Let the seeds soak overnight in a dark cupboard (away from light).

6   In the morning, pour off all the water, making sure none of it pools inside. You can leave the jar (with the cheesecloth still intact) upside down on a plate or bowl to ensure drainage.

7   Hold the drained jar horizontally and shake gently to distribute the seeds along the side of the jar. Place on its side and cover with a dishtowel to block out light for about 4 hours.

8   Rinse the jar with fresh water two or three times a day, every day. Drain each time and set the jar back on its side.

9   The sprouts should be ready to harvest in 3 to 5 days. Taste them after every rinse to see when the flavor has developed to your taste.

10 Fill the jar with water for the last time and remove any thick hulls (the outer covering of the seeds).

11 Drain the sprouts in a colander and eat immediately, or wrap in a single layer of dishtowel or paper towel and hold in the refrigerator, where they will keep for 4 to 7 days.

Homegrown Sprouts

- Alfalfa
- Broccoli
- Chickpea
- Leek
- Lentil

- Mung bean
- Onion
- Pea
- Red clover
- Sunflower

GROWING YOUR FOOD SCRAPS
A.K.A. GROCERY STORE PROPAGATION

Extending the life of any vegetable is the ultimate nod toward living sustainably and with environmental consciousness, so why not continue benefiting from food you purchased or grew? Get the most out of all vegetables before sending them to the compost bin by cultivating a food scrap garden on your windowsill or countertop.

Plants grow. They are living things and will continue to grow roots and sprouts even after harvest. We've all seen this when a potato left too long in our pantry sprouts, or the garlic cloves send up green shoots. Most plants will continue to grow even without soil, needing only water, sunlight, and eventually food to continue producing. This works particularly well for anything with a leafy green that we can harvest.

Leaves grow from the center out and will put on growth slowly, so don't expect to get great harvests from this foray into growing from scraps. It's a fun project that ensures you'll always have *something* fresh at hand, and a great way to involve kids in urban agriculture and nutrition.

The process is pretty straightforward and simple. The basic how-to involves setting the root end of a vegetable in a shallow bowl of water and placing it in a sunny spot—a windowsill that receives direct sun is the perfect setting. You can use a tall water glass, a shallow baking pan, or any receptacle in which the vegetable can stand in a shallow pool of water. Standing water is a hospitable atmosphere for bacteria and encourages decomposition, so be sure to change out the water and clean the dish regularly—once every two to three days, at least.

I suggest starting with a locally grown, organic vegetable because these are typically cultivated as a field crop in healthy soils and spend less time in transport, making them a healthier choice all around.

Celery and Bok Choy

Trim the edible portions from a head of celery or bok choy, cutting 2 inches above the root end. If the cut root end of the plant is soft and browned, slice off a very thin layer. Set the root base in a tall glass and fill with enough water so the bottom ¼ to ½ inch of root is submerged.

Herbs

Many tender herbs will develop root systems from the stem if planted into soil as a cutting or left in a shallow glass of water. (Many flowering plants will do this—zinnia, lilac, and geranium, to name a few.) Try mint and basil. (Note: cilantro and parsley are exceptions; they do not root and grow from cuttings.) To grow, cut just below a set of leaves and then remove the lower leaves. Woody herbs, like rosemary, are a bit trickier—use a fresh cutting from new growth (see Propagation in the Seeds, Seed Starting, and Propagation chapter, page 86), but they won't quickly develop new leaf sets for harvesting.

Lettuce

Choose a nonheading lettuce for this project; crispheads like iceberg lettuces do not work well. As with celery, trim the bulk of the leaves from the stem, leaving behind about 2 inches on the root end of the plant. If the root end of the plant is soft and browned, slice off a very thin layer. Set the root base in a tall glass and fill with enough water so the last ¼ to ½ inch of root is submerged, and place in a sunny spot.

Green Onions/Scallions

Trim the edible, green portion from the tall onions, leaving behind about 2 inches of stem on the root end of the plant. Set the root base in a tall glass and fill with enough water so the last ¼ to ½ inch of root is submerged. The green tops will regrow for several weeks (don't forget to change the water!), and you can continue cutting them and regrowing them until production slows.

Tubers: Potatoes, Ginger, Turmeric

The edible parts of these plants are grown underground as a tuber. A quick note on growing these plants from scraps. Can you do it? Sort of. You just use a piece of the food as a starting point for a new plant. To give this a try, cut pieces from the tuber and float them in a shallow pool of water until they develop root systems; then you can plant them deeply in soil.

Mushrooms

Yes, you can grow your own mushrooms, on a countertop or outdoors. In recent years, mushroom growers have started offering grow-your-own mushroom kits, making it easy to grow delicious fungi at home. Any kit you purchase will have detailed instructions about how to get them started and keep them going through multiple harvests.

Kits are available for common varieties like shiitake and oyster mushrooms and more coveted varieties like lion's mane and reishi. The kits are shipped with a growing medium and, more often than not, decaying pieces of log that are then inoculated with mushroom spores.

How to Dry Herbs

Drying herbs (or most edibles for that matter) is a satisfying project and the perfect way to extend your harvest. Herbs put out growth quite quickly. Combine fast-growing plants with busy lifestyles, and many home gardeners find they aren't home enough to use fresh-cut herbs in time. These plants also do better when you are actively cutting from them and stimulating them to put on new growth. I often see herbs go to flower when they should be cut back and used in cooking instead. When your herbs are growing faster than you're able to incorporate them into your meals, it's time to turn to herb drying.

To dry out fresh herbs, choose a warm, dry place. Molds, bacteria, and yeast all thrive in moisture and can ruin herb-saving projects, so keep drying herbs free from excess moisture. Cut herbs down almost to the root, making certain to leave some green leaves and room for them to continue growing. (General harvesting tips can be found in the What to Grow for a Plentiful Harvest chapter.) There are two methods for drying herbs: hanging or tray drying. For hanging herbs, tie the stems together and hang from a hook in the ceiling until dry. For tray drying, place the herb cuttings on a parchment-lined baking sheet and turn them occasionally so moisture does not collect under the leaves. Most herbs should dry out in four to six days. They are fully dry when they crumble easily to the touch.

Resources

There is a wealth of information available for anyone interested in food, growing food, and cooking at home; these are some of my favorite resources that I reference time and time again. These sources get to the heart of the matter and provide enough information for you to make your own decisions about gardening, small urban farm projects, preserving, and cooking.

GROWING FOOD AT HOME

My Website and Newsletter
Amy-Pennington.com
Articles, tips, and tricks about all things homegrown.

Rodale's Ultimate Encyclopedia of Organic Gardening
By the editor of *Organic Gardening and Farming Magazine* (New York: Rodale, 2009). I have the vintage version (*The Encyclopedia of Organic Gardening*, 1976), passed down from my father. It is a must for scientific plant information.

Seed Sources:

Johnny's Selected Seeds
JohnnySeeds.com
An excellent one-stop shop for seeds, they carry pretty much anything you'll need.

Mushroom Kits
CascadiaMushrooms.com and *FieldForest.net*

Organic Seed Alliance
SeedAlliance.org
A great resource for locating organic seed for veggies and flowers.

Potatoes

TerritorialSeed.com and
MainePotatoLady.com
Good resources for both East
Coast and West Coast gardeners.

Scented Geraniums

MountainValleyGrowers.com
Here is one of the few resources
with a bounty of scented
geraniums, and you can order
online and have plants shipped.

Seed Savers Exchange

Exchange.SeedSavers.org
Save our seeds! Seeds are a
precious resource—learn how to
save them and share with others.

URBAN HOMESTEADING

Quillisascut School of the Domestic Arts

Quillisascut.com
Worth the trip to Washington's
farm country, "Quilla" changed
my life. They offer week-long farm
immersions and workshops to
introduce and connect people to
their food.

COOKING AND FOOD

Farmers' Markets and Local Food Marketing

www.ams.usda.gov/local-food-directories/farmersmarkets
Support your local food
producers and small family farms!

PRESERVING FOOD

Cooperative Extension Programs

https://nifa.usda.gov/extension
Find your local program, and
you'll find a *ton* of useful
information about home
food preservation and local
agriculture.

National Center for Home Food Preservation

www.uga.edu/nchfp
All the rules you could ever
hope to know about safe home
canning—plus some decent
recipes!

Acknowledgments

I would like to thank my daddio, Seth Dorian Pennington, Jr., for having an insatiable verve for living off the land, so much so that in retirement he moved himself and a herd of goats out to the countryside of Pennsylvania and nestled them all against the banks of a mountain-fed stream.

Thank you to the team at Sasquatch Books who kept our garden conversation alive and well over many growing seasons, and most especially to Susan Roxborough, Tony Ong, Anna Goldstein, and Jill Saginario. And a special thank you to Whitney Ricketts for yelling at me over a martini to "Write the damn book, already!"

Super big fat thank-you to Della Chen and Charity Burggraaf, the photographers of this book and world-class creative humans.

I owe a huge, huge thank-you to Patric Gabre-Kidan, one of my very best friends and an overall Mr. Fix-It who has been the most incredible teacher over the years. He has single-handedly taught me how to change a tire, hold a chef's knife properly, and build my own vegetable planter box. He is my superhero.

I have so much gratitude for Lucio and Marta Dalla Gasparina, who had the excellent idea that I should grow their nonna's Italian tomatoes in their yard for them. They didn't know they were creating a monster and lighting a spark in my life, and for that I am eternally grateful.

Double special thanks to Lynda Oosterhuis for always sharing her cooking secrets. She is one of the most amazing cooks I know.

As always, thank you to my family: Mom, Stacy, Seth, Gram, and the gaggle of nieces and nephews who crack me up daily. Love and thanks to my BK family: David, Carol, Dan, and Lil. This new edition is for a new baby, Wylie. May you always live green.

And finally, thank you to anyone reading these thank-yous! Your interest in and support of all things urban farm and garden are utterly inspiring. Keep growing!

Index

Note: Page numbers in *italic* refer to photographs.

Printed in China

SASQUATCH BOOKS with colophon is a registered trademark of Penguin Random House LLC

26 25 24 23 22   9 8 7 6 5 4 3 2 1

Editor: Susan Roxborough   Production editor: Jill Saginario   Designer: Tony Ong

Photo credits: Cover © SimonidaDjordjevic/iStockPhoto.com, endsheets © Charity Burggraaf, pg. ii © Anja Schaefer/Alamy.com, pg. iv © RDonar/DepositPhotos.com, pg. vi © Charity Burggraaf, pg. xii © Della Chen, pg. 4 © Della Chen, pg. 8 © Della Chen, pg. 14 © Ina Peters/Stocksy.com, pg. 23 © Olga Romankova/Stock.Adobe.com, pg. 32 © Westend61 GmbH/Alamy.com, pg. 38 © Redmark/iStockPhoto.com, pg. 42 © Melissa Ross/Stocksy.com, pg. 46 © Mathias Podstawka/Alamy.com, pg. 49 © Nito/Alamy.com, pg. 51 © Nataša Mandić/Stocksy.com, pg. 53 © Jiri Vaclavek/Dreamstime.com, pg. 56 © Charity Burggraaf, pg. 58 © Charity Burggraaf, pg. 70 © Charity Burggraaf, pg. 76 © Chernetskaya/Dreamstime.com, pg. 90 © Sandra Cunningham/Stocksy.com, pg. 103 © Della Chen, pg. 110 © Charity Burggraaf, pg. 115 © Della Chen, pg. 116 © Charity Burggraaf, pg. 118 © Della Chen, pg. 120 © Della Chen, pg. 127 © Charity Burggraaf, pg. 131 © Della Chen, pg. 132 © Charity Burggraaf, pg. 138 © Charity Burggraaf, pg. 142 © Charity Burggraaf, pg. 147 © Della Chen, pg. 148 © Charity Burggraaf, pg. 152 © Charity Burggraaf, pg. 156 © Charity Burggraaf, pg. 160 © Charity Burggraaf, pg. 165 © Della Chen, pg. 167 © Veera/Stock.Adobe.com, pg. 169 © Charity Burggraaf, pg. 172 © Della Chen, pg. 176 © Charity Burggraaf, pg. 180 © Della Chen, pg. 184 © RobynMac/iStockPhoto.com, pg. 190 © Charity Burggraaf

Library of Congress Cataloging-in-Publication Data is available.

ISBN: 978-1-63217-392-8

Sasquatch Books | 1904 Third Avenue, Suite 710
Seattle, WA 98101 | SasquatchBooks.com

MIX
Paper from
responsible sources
FSC® C001701